C-3433 CAREER EXAMINATION SERIES

This is your
PASSBOOK for...

Child Support Specialist

Test Preparation Study Guide
Questions & Answers

COPYRIGHT NOTICE

This book is SOLELY intended for, is sold ONLY to, and its use is RESTRICTED to individual, bona fide applicants or candidates who qualify by virtue of having seriously filed applications for appropriate license, certificate, professional and/or promotional advancement, higher school matriculation, scholarship, or other legitimate requirements of education and/or governmental authorities.

This book is NOT intended for use, class instruction, tutoring, training, duplication, copying, reprinting, excerption, or adaptation, etc., by:

1) Other publishers
2) Proprietors and/or Instructors of "Coaching" and/or Preparatory Courses
3) Personnel and/or Training Divisions of commercial, industrial, and governmental organizations
4) Schools, colleges, or universities and/or their departments and staffs, including teachers and other personnel
5) Testing Agencies or Bureaus
6) Study groups which seek by the purchase of a single volume to copy and/or duplicate and/or adapt this material for use by the group as a whole without having purchased individual volumes for each of the members of the group
7) Et al.

Such persons would be in violation of appropriate Federal and State statutes.

PROVISION OF LICENSING AGREEMENTS – Recognized educational, commercial, industrial, and governmental institutions and organizations, and others legitimately engaged in educational pursuits, including training, testing, and measurement activities, may address request for a licensing agreement to the copyright owners, who will determine whether, and under what conditions, including fees and charges, the materials in this book may be used them. In other words, a licensing facility exists for the legitimate use of the material in this book on other than an individual basis. However, it is asseverated and affirmed here that the material in this book CANNOT be used without the receipt of the express permission of such a licensing agreement from the Publishers. Inquiries re licensing should be addressed to the company, attention rights and permissions department.

All rights reserved, including the right of reproduction in whole or in part, in any form or by any means, electronic or mechanical, including photocopying, recording, or by any information storage and retrieval system, without permission in writing from the Publisher.

Copyright © 2024 by
National Learning Corporation

212 Michael Drive, Syosset, NY 11791
(516) 921-8888 • www.passbooks.com
E-mail: info@passbooks.com

PUBLISHED IN THE UNITED STATES OF AMERICA

PASSBOOK® SERIES

THE *PASSBOOK® SERIES* has been created to prepare applicants and candidates for the ultimate academic battlefield – the examination room.

At some time in our lives, each and every one of us may be required to take an examination – for validation, matriculation, admission, qualification, registration, certification, or licensure.

Based on the assumption that every applicant or candidate has met the basic formal educational standards, has taken the required number of courses, and read the necessary texts, the *PASSBOOK® SERIES* furnishes the one special preparation which may assure passing with confidence, instead of failing with insecurity. Examination questions – together with answers – are furnished as the basic vehicle for study so that the mysteries of the examination and its compounding difficulties may be eliminated or diminished by a sure method.

This book is meant to help you pass your examination provided that you qualify and are serious in your objective.

The entire field is reviewed through the huge store of content information which is succinctly presented through a provocative and challenging approach – the question-and-answer method.

A climate of success is established by furnishing the correct answers at the end of each test.

You soon learn to recognize types of questions, forms of questions, and patterns of questioning. You may even begin to anticipate expected outcomes.

You perceive that many questions are repeated or adapted so that you can gain acute insights, which may enable you to score many sure points.

You learn how to confront new questions, or types of questions, and to attack them confidently and work out the correct answers.

You note objectives and emphases, and recognize pitfalls and dangers, so that you may make positive educational adjustments.

Moreover, you are kept fully informed in relation to new concepts, methods, practices, and directions in the field.

You discover that you are actually taking the examination all the time: you are preparing for the examination by "taking" an examination, not by reading extraneous and/or supererogatory textbooks.

In short, this PASSBOOK®, used directedly, should be an important factor in helping you to pass your test.

CHILD SUPPORT SPECIALIST

DUTIES
Responsible for conducting investigations to locate individuals legally responsible for the support of dependents so that support and paternity orders may be established and payments obtained through voluntary agreement or court orders. Duties may include: monitoring and providing technical assistance to local districts to improve their child support performance; developing and monitoring child support related contracts; and drafting policy and procedures. Performs related work as required.

SCOPE OF THE EXAMINATION
The written test will cover knowledge, skills and/or abilities in such areas as:

1. Investigating and analyzing financial resources;
2. Understanding and interpreting written material, including laws, documents and procedures;
3. Interviewing;
4. Preparing written material;
5. Understanding and interpreting tabular material; and
6. Arithmetic reasoning.

HOW TO TAKE A TEST

I. YOU MUST PASS AN EXAMINATION

A. *WHAT EVERY CANDIDATE SHOULD KNOW*

Examination applicants often ask us for help in preparing for the written test. What can I study in advance? What kinds of questions will be asked? How will the test be given? How will the papers be graded?

As an applicant for a civil service examination, you may be wondering about some of these things. Our purpose here is to suggest effective methods of advance study and to describe civil service examinations.

Your chances for success on this examination can be increased if you know how to prepare. Those "pre-examination jitters" can be reduced if you know what to expect. You can even experience an adventure in good citizenship if you know why civil service exams are given.

B. *WHY ARE CIVIL SERVICE EXAMINATIONS GIVEN?*

Civil service examinations are important to you in two ways. As a citizen, you want public jobs filled by employees who know how to do their work. As a job seeker, you want a fair chance to compete for that job on an equal footing with other candidates. The best-known means of accomplishing this two-fold goal is the competitive examination.

Exams are widely publicized throughout the nation. They may be administered for jobs in federal, state, city, municipal, town or village governments or agencies.

Any citizen may apply, with some limitations, such as the age or residence of applicants. Your experience and education may be reviewed to see whether you meet the requirements for the particular examination. When these requirements exist, they are reasonable and applied consistently to all applicants. Thus, a competitive examination may cause you some uneasiness now, but it is your privilege and safeguard.

C. *HOW ARE CIVIL SERVICE EXAMS DEVELOPED?*

Examinations are carefully written by trained technicians who are specialists in the field known as "psychological measurement," in consultation with recognized authorities in the field of work that the test will cover. These experts recommend the subject matter areas or skills to be tested; only those knowledges or skills important to your success on the job are included. The most reliable books and source materials available are used as references. Together, the experts and technicians judge the difficulty level of the questions.

Test technicians know how to phrase questions so that the problem is clearly stated. Their ethics do not permit "trick" or "catch" questions. Questions may have been tried out on sample groups, or subjected to statistical analysis, to determine their usefulness.

Written tests are often used in combination with performance tests, ratings of training and experience, and oral interviews. All of these measures combine to form the best-known means of finding the right person for the right job.

II. HOW TO PASS THE WRITTEN TEST

A. NATURE OF THE EXAMINATION

To prepare intelligently for civil service examinations, you should know how they differ from school examinations you have taken. In school you were assigned certain definite pages to read or subjects to cover. The examination questions were quite detailed and usually emphasized memory. Civil service exams, on the other hand, try to discover your present ability to perform the duties of a position, plus your potentiality to learn these duties. In other words, a civil service exam attempts to predict how successful you will be. Questions cover such a broad area that they cannot be as minute and detailed as school exam questions.

In the public service similar kinds of work, or positions, are grouped together in one "class." This process is known as *position-classification*. All the positions in a class are paid according to the salary range for that class. One class title covers all of these positions, and they are all tested by the same examination.

B. FOUR BASIC STEPS

1) Study the announcement

How, then, can you know what subjects to study? Our best answer is: "Learn as much as possible about the class of positions for which you've applied." The exam will test the knowledge, skills and abilities needed to do the work.

Your most valuable source of information about the position you want is the official exam announcement. This announcement lists the training and experience qualifications. Check these standards and apply only if you come reasonably close to meeting them.

The brief description of the position in the examination announcement offers some clues to the subjects which will be tested. Think about the job itself. Review the duties in your mind. Can you perform them, or are there some in which you are rusty? Fill in the blank spots in your preparation.

Many jurisdictions preview the written test in the exam announcement by including a section called "Knowledge and Abilities Required," "Scope of the Examination," or some similar heading. Here you will find out specifically what fields will be tested.

2) Review your own background

Once you learn in general what the position is all about, and what you need to know to do the work, ask yourself which subjects you already know fairly well and which need improvement. You may wonder whether to concentrate on improving your strong areas or on building some background in your fields of weakness. When the announcement has specified "some knowledge" or "considerable knowledge," or has used adjectives like "beginning principles of..." or "advanced ... methods," you can get a clue as to the number and difficulty of questions to be asked in any given field. More questions, and hence broader coverage, would be included for those subjects which are more important in the work. Now weigh your strengths and weaknesses against the job requirements and prepare accordingly.

3) Determine the level of the position

Another way to tell how intensively you should prepare is to understand the level of the job for which you are applying. Is it the entering level? In other words, is this the position in which beginners in a field of work are hired? Or is it an intermediate or advanced level? Sometimes this is indicated by such words as "Junior" or "Senior" in the class title. Other jurisdictions use Roman numerals to designate the level – Clerk I, Clerk II, for example. The word "Supervisor" sometimes appears in the title. If the level is not indicated by the title, check the description of duties. Will you be working under very close supervision, or will you have responsibility for independent decisions in this work?

4) Choose appropriate study materials

Now that you know the subjects to be examined and the relative amount of each subject to be covered, you can choose suitable study materials. For beginning level jobs, or even advanced ones, if you have a pronounced weakness in some aspect of your training, read a modern, standard textbook in that field. Be sure it is up to date and has general coverage. Such books are normally available at your library, and the librarian will be glad to help you locate one. For entry-level positions, questions of appropriate difficulty are chosen – neither highly advanced questions, nor those too simple. Such questions require careful thought but not advanced training.

If the position for which you are applying is technical or advanced, you will read more advanced, specialized material. If you are already familiar with the basic principles of your field, elementary textbooks would waste your time. Concentrate on advanced textbooks and technical periodicals. Think through the concepts and review difficult problems in your field.

These are all general sources. You can get more ideas on your own initiative, following these leads. For example, training manuals and publications of the government agency which employs workers in your field can be useful, particularly for technical and professional positions. A letter or visit to the government department involved may result in more specific study suggestions, and certainly will provide you with a more definite idea of the exact nature of the position you are seeking.

III. KINDS OF TESTS

Tests are used for purposes other than measuring knowledge and ability to perform specified duties. For some positions, it is equally important to test ability to make adjustments to new situations or to profit from training. In others, basic mental abilities not dependent on information are essential. Questions which test these things may not appear as pertinent to the duties of the position as those which test for knowledge and information. Yet they are often highly important parts of a fair examination. For very general questions, it is almost impossible to help you direct your study efforts. What we can do is to point out some of the more common of these general abilities needed in public service positions and describe some typical questions.

1) General information

Broad, general information has been found useful for predicting job success in some kinds of work. This is tested in a variety of ways, from vocabulary lists to questions about current events. Basic background in some field of work, such as sociology or economics, may be sampled in a group of questions. Often these are principles which have become familiar to most persons through exposure rather than through formal training. It is difficult to advise you how to study for these questions; being alert to the world around you is our best suggestion.

2) Verbal ability

An example of an ability needed in many positions is verbal or language ability. Verbal ability is, in brief, the ability to use and understand words. Vocabulary and grammar tests are typical measures of this ability. Reading comprehension or paragraph interpretation questions are common in many kinds of civil service tests. You are given a paragraph of written material and asked to find its central meaning.

3) Numerical ability

Number skills can be tested by the familiar arithmetic problem, by checking paired lists of numbers to see which are alike and which are different, or by interpreting charts and graphs. In the latter test, a graph may be printed in the test booklet which you are asked to use as the basis for answering questions.

4) Observation

A popular test for law-enforcement positions is the observation test. A picture is shown to you for several minutes, then taken away. Questions about the picture test your ability to observe both details and larger elements.

5) Following directions

In many positions in the public service, the employee must be able to carry out written instructions dependably and accurately. You may be given a chart with several columns, each column listing a variety of information. The questions require you to carry out directions involving the information given in the chart.

6) Skills and aptitudes

Performance tests effectively measure some manual skills and aptitudes. When the skill is one in which you are trained, such as typing or shorthand, you can practice. These tests are often very much like those given in business school or high school courses. For many of the other skills and aptitudes, however, no short-time preparation can be made. Skills and abilities natural to you or that you have developed throughout your lifetime are being tested.

Many of the general questions just described provide all the data needed to answer the questions and ask you to use your reasoning ability to find the answers. Your best preparation for these tests, as well as for tests of facts and ideas, is to be at your physical and mental best. You, no doubt, have your own methods of getting into an exam-taking mood and keeping "in shape." The next section lists some ideas on this subject.

IV. KINDS OF QUESTIONS

Only rarely is the "essay" question, which you answer in narrative form, used in civil service tests. Civil service tests are usually of the short-answer type. Full instructions for answering these questions will be given to you at the examination. But in case this is your first experience with short-answer questions and separate answer sheets, here is what you need to know:

1) Multiple-choice Questions

Most popular of the short-answer questions is the "multiple choice" or "best answer" question. It can be used, for example, to test for factual knowledge, ability to solve problems or judgment in meeting situations found at work.

A multiple-choice question is normally one of three types—
- It can begin with an incomplete statement followed by several possible endings. You are to find the one ending which *best* completes the statement, although some of the others may not be entirely wrong.
- It can also be a complete statement in the form of a question which is answered by choosing one of the statements listed.

- It can be in the form of a problem – again you select the best answer.

Here is an example of a multiple-choice question with a discussion which should give you some clues as to the method for choosing the right answer:

When an employee has a complaint about his assignment, the action which will *best* help him overcome his difficulty is to
- A. discuss his difficulty with his coworkers
- B. take the problem to the head of the organization
- C. take the problem to the person who gave him the assignment
- D. say nothing to anyone about his complaint

In answering this question, you should study each of the choices to find which is best. Consider choice "A" – Certainly an employee may discuss his complaint with fellow employees, but no change or improvement can result, and the complaint remains unresolved. Choice "B" is a poor choice since the head of the organization probably does not know what assignment you have been given, and taking your problem to him is known as "going over the head" of the supervisor. The supervisor, or person who made the assignment, is the person who can clarify it or correct any injustice. Choice "C" is, therefore, correct. To say nothing, as in choice "D," is unwise. Supervisors have and interest in knowing the problems employees are facing, and the employee is seeking a solution to his problem.

2) True/False Questions

The "true/false" or "right/wrong" form of question is sometimes used. Here a complete statement is given. Your job is to decide whether the statement is right or wrong.

SAMPLE: A roaming cell-phone call to a nearby city costs less than a non-roaming call to a distant city.

This statement is wrong, or false, since roaming calls are more expensive.

This is not a complete list of all possible question forms, although most of the others are variations of these common types. You will always get complete directions for answering questions. Be sure you understand *how* to mark your answers – ask questions until you do.

V. RECORDING YOUR ANSWERS

Computer terminals are used more and more today for many different kinds of exams.

For an examination with very few applicants, you may be told to record your answers in the test booklet itself. Separate answer sheets are much more common. If this separate answer sheet is to be scored by machine – and this is often the case – it is highly important that you mark your answers correctly in order to get credit.

An electronic scoring machine is often used in civil service offices because of the speed with which papers can be scored. Machine-scored answer sheets must be marked with a pencil, which will be given to you. This pencil has a high graphite content which responds to the electronic scoring machine. As a matter of fact, stray dots may register as answers, so do not let your pencil rest on the answer sheet while you are pondering the correct answer. Also, if your pencil lead breaks or is otherwise defective, ask for another.

Since the answer sheet will be dropped in a slot in the scoring machine, be careful not to bend the corners or get the paper crumpled.

The answer sheet normally has five vertical columns of numbers, with 30 numbers to a column. These numbers correspond to the question numbers in your test booklet. After each number, going across the page are four or five pairs of dotted lines. These short dotted lines have small letters or numbers above them. The first two pairs may also have a "T" or "F" above the letters. This indicates that the first two pairs only are to be used if the questions are of the true-false type. If the questions are multiple choice, disregard the "T" and "F" and pay attention only to the small letters or numbers.

Answer your questions in the manner of the sample that follows:

32. The largest city in the United States is
   A. Washington, D.C.
   B. New York City
   C. Chicago
   D. Detroit
   E. San Francisco

1) Choose the answer you think is best. (New York City is the largest, so "B" is correct.)
2) Find the row of dotted lines numbered the same as the question you are answering. (Find row number 32)
3) Find the pair of dotted lines corresponding to the answer. (Find the pair of lines under the mark "B.")
4) Make a solid black mark between the dotted lines.

VI. BEFORE THE TEST

Common sense will help you find procedures to follow to get ready for an examination. Too many of us, however, overlook these sensible measures. Indeed, nervousness and fatigue have been found to be the most serious reasons why applicants fail to do their best on civil service tests. Here is a list of reminders:

- Begin your preparation early – Don't wait until the last minute to go scurrying around for books and materials or to find out what the position is all about.
- Prepare continuously – An hour a night for a week is better than an all-night cram session. This has been definitely established. What is more, a night a week for a month will return better dividends than crowding your study into a shorter period of time.
- Locate the place of the exam – You have been sent a notice telling you when and where to report for the examination. If the location is in a different town or otherwise unfamiliar to you, it would be well to inquire the best route and learn something about the building.
- Relax the night before the test – Allow your mind to rest. Do not study at all that night. Plan some mild recreation or diversion; then go to bed early and get a good night's sleep.
- Get up early enough to make a leisurely trip to the place for the test – This way unforeseen events, traffic snarls, unfamiliar buildings, etc. will not upset you.
- Dress comfortably – A written test is not a fashion show. You will be known by number and not by name, so wear something comfortable.

- Leave excess paraphernalia at home – Shopping bags and odd bundles will get in your way. You need bring only the items mentioned in the official notice you received; usually everything you need is provided. Do not bring reference books to the exam. They will only confuse those last minutes and be taken away from you when in the test room.
- Arrive somewhat ahead of time – If because of transportation schedules you must get there very early, bring a newspaper or magazine to take your mind off yourself while waiting.
- Locate the examination room – When you have found the proper room, you will be directed to the seat or part of the room where you will sit. Sometimes you are given a sheet of instructions to read while you are waiting. Do not fill out any forms until you are told to do so; just read them and be prepared.
- Relax and prepare to listen to the instructions
- If you have any physical problem that may keep you from doing your best, be sure to tell the test administrator. If you are sick or in poor health, you really cannot do your best on the exam. You can come back and take the test some other time.

VII. AT THE TEST

The day of the test is here and you have the test booklet in your hand. The temptation to get going is very strong. Caution! There is more to success than knowing the right answers. You must know how to identify your papers and understand variations in the type of short-answer question used in this particular examination. Follow these suggestions for maximum results from your efforts:

1) Cooperate with the monitor

The test administrator has a duty to create a situation in which you can be as much at ease as possible. He will give instructions, tell you when to begin, check to see that you are marking your answer sheet correctly, and so on. He is not there to guard you, although he will see that your competitors do not take unfair advantage. He wants to help you do your best.

2) Listen to all instructions

Don't jump the gun! Wait until you understand all directions. In most civil service tests you get more time than you need to answer the questions. So don't be in a hurry. Read each word of instructions until you clearly understand the meaning. Study the examples, listen to all announcements and follow directions. Ask questions if you do not understand what to do.

3) Identify your papers

Civil service exams are usually identified by number only. You will be assigned a number; you must not put your name on your test papers. Be sure to copy your number correctly. Since more than one exam may be given, copy your exact examination title.

4) Plan your time

Unless you are told that a test is a "speed" or "rate of work" test, speed itself is usually not important. Time enough to answer all the questions will be provided, but this does not mean that you have all day. An overall time limit has been set. Divide the total time (in minutes) by the number of questions to determine the approximate time you have for each question.

5) Do not linger over difficult questions

If you come across a difficult question, mark it with a paper clip (useful to have along) and come back to it when you have been through the booklet. One caution if you do this – be sure to skip a number on your answer sheet as well. Check often to be sure that you have not lost your place and that you are marking in the row numbered the same as the question you are answering.

6) Read the questions

Be sure you know what the question asks! Many capable people are unsuccessful because they failed to *read* the questions correctly.

7) Answer all questions

Unless you have been instructed that a penalty will be deducted for incorrect answers, it is better to guess than to omit a question.

8) Speed tests

It is often better NOT to guess on speed tests. It has been found that on timed tests people are tempted to spend the last few seconds before time is called in marking answers at random – without even reading them – in the hope of picking up a few extra points. To discourage this practice, the instructions may warn you that your score will be "corrected" for guessing. That is, a penalty will be applied. The incorrect answers will be deducted from the correct ones, or some other penalty formula will be used.

9) Review your answers

If you finish before time is called, go back to the questions you guessed or omitted to give them further thought. Review other answers if you have time.

10) Return your test materials

If you are ready to leave before others have finished or time is called, take ALL your materials to the monitor and leave quietly. Never take any test material with you. The monitor can discover whose papers are not complete, and taking a test booklet may be grounds for disqualification.

VIII. EXAMINATION TECHNIQUES

1) Read the general instructions carefully. These are usually printed on the first page of the exam booklet. As a rule, these instructions refer to the timing of the examination; the fact that you should not start work until the signal and must stop work at a signal, etc. If there are any *special* instructions, such as a choice of questions to be answered, make sure that you note this instruction carefully.

2) When you are ready to start work on the examination, that is as soon as the signal has been given, read the instructions to each question booklet, underline any key words or phrases, such as *least, best, outline, describe* and the like. In this way you will tend to answer as requested rather than discover on reviewing your paper that you *listed without describing*, that you selected the *worst* choice rather than the *best* choice, etc.

3) If the examination is of the objective or multiple-choice type – that is, each question will also give a series of possible answers: A, B, C or D, and you are called upon to select the best answer and write the letter next to that answer on your answer paper – it is advisable to start answering each question in turn. There may be anywhere from 50 to 100 such questions in the three or four hours allotted and you can see how much time would be taken if you read through all the questions before beginning to answer any. Furthermore, if you come across a question or group of questions which you know would be difficult to answer, it would undoubtedly affect your handling of all the other questions.

4) If the examination is of the essay type and contains but a few questions, it is a moot point as to whether you should read all the questions before starting to answer any one. Of course, if you are given a choice – say five out of seven and the like – then it is essential to read all the questions so you can eliminate the two that are most difficult. If, however, you are asked to answer all the questions, there may be danger in trying to answer the easiest one first because you may find that you will spend too much time on it. The best technique is to answer the first question, then proceed to the second, etc.

5) Time your answers. Before the exam begins, write down the time it started, then add the time allowed for the examination and write down the time it must be completed, then divide the time available somewhat as follows:
   - If 3-1/2 hours are allowed, that would be 210 minutes. If you have 80 objective-type questions, that would be an average of 2-1/2 minutes per question. Allow yourself no more than 2 minutes per question, or a total of 160 minutes, which will permit about 50 minutes to review.
   - If for the time allotment of 210 minutes there are 7 essay questions to answer, that would average about 30 minutes a question. Give yourself only 25 minutes per question so that you have about 35 minutes to review.

6) The most important instruction is to *read each question* and make sure you know what is wanted. The second most important instruction is to *time yourself properly* so that you answer every question. The third most important instruction is to *answer every question*. Guess if you have to but include something for each question. Remember that you will receive no credit for a blank and will probably receive some credit if you write something in answer to an essay question. If you guess a letter – say "B" for a multiple-choice question – you may have guessed right. If you leave a blank as an answer to a multiple-choice question, the examiners may respect your feelings but it will not add a point to your score. Some exams may penalize you for wrong answers, so in such cases *only*, you may not want to guess unless you have some basis for your answer.

7) Suggestions
   a. Objective-type questions
      1. Examine the question booklet for proper sequence of pages and questions
      2. Read all instructions carefully
      3. Skip any question which seems too difficult; return to it after all other questions have been answered
      4. Apportion your time properly; do not spend too much time on any single question or group of questions

5. Note and underline key words – *all, most, fewest, least, best, worst, same, opposite,* etc.
6. Pay particular attention to negatives
7. Note unusual option, e.g., unduly long, short, complex, different or similar in content to the body of the question
8. Observe the use of "hedging" words – *probably, may, most likely,* etc.
9. Make sure that your answer is put next to the same number as the question
10. Do not second-guess unless you have good reason to believe the second answer is definitely more correct
11. Cross out original answer if you decide another answer is more accurate; do not erase until you are ready to hand your paper in
12. Answer all questions; guess unless instructed otherwise
13. Leave time for review

b. Essay questions
1. Read each question carefully
2. Determine exactly what is wanted. Underline key words or phrases.
3. Decide on outline or paragraph answer
4. Include many different points and elements unless asked to develop any one or two points or elements
5. Show impartiality by giving pros and cons unless directed to select one side only
6. Make and write down any assumptions you find necessary to answer the questions
7. Watch your English, grammar, punctuation and choice of words
8. Time your answers; don't crowd material

8) Answering the essay question

Most essay questions can be answered by framing the specific response around several key words or ideas. Here are a few such key words or ideas:

M's: manpower, materials, methods, money, management
P's: purpose, program, policy, plan, procedure, practice, problems, pitfalls, personnel, public relations

a. Six basic steps in handling problems:
1. Preliminary plan and background development
2. Collect information, data and facts
3. Analyze and interpret information, data and facts
4. Analyze and develop solutions as well as make recommendations
5. Prepare report and sell recommendations
6. Install recommendations and follow up effectiveness

b. Pitfalls to avoid
1. *Taking things for granted* – A statement of the situation does not necessarily imply that each of the elements is necessarily true; for example, a complaint may be invalid and biased so that all that can be taken for granted is that a complaint has been registered

2. *Considering only one side of a situation* – Wherever possible, indicate several alternatives and then point out the reasons you selected the best one
3. *Failing to indicate follow up* – Whenever your answer indicates action on your part, make certain that you will take proper follow-up action to see how successful your recommendations, procedures or actions turn out to be
4. *Taking too long in answering any single question* – Remember to time your answers properly

IX. AFTER THE TEST

Scoring procedures differ in detail among civil service jurisdictions although the general principles are the same. Whether the papers are hand-scored or graded by machine we have described, they are nearly always graded by number. That is, the person who marks the paper knows only the number – never the name – of the applicant. Not until all the papers have been graded will they be matched with names. If other tests, such as training and experience or oral interview ratings have been given, scores will be combined. Different parts of the examination usually have different weights. For example, the written test might count 60 percent of the final grade, and a rating of training and experience 40 percent. In many jurisdictions, veterans will have a certain number of points added to their grades.

After the final grade has been determined, the names are placed in grade order and an eligible list is established. There are various methods for resolving ties between those who get the same final grade – probably the most common is to place first the name of the person whose application was received first. Job offers are made from the eligible list in the order the names appear on it. You will be notified of your grade and your rank as soon as all these computations have been made. This will be done as rapidly as possible.

People who are found to meet the requirements in the announcement are called "eligibles." Their names are put on a list of eligible candidates. An eligible's chances of getting a job depend on how high he stands on this list and how fast agencies are filling jobs from the list.

When a job is to be filled from a list of eligibles, the agency asks for the names of people on the list of eligibles for that job. When the civil service commission receives this request, it sends to the agency the names of the three people highest on this list. Or, if the job to be filled has specialized requirements, the office sends the agency the names of the top three persons who meet these requirements from the general list.

The appointing officer makes a choice from among the three people whose names were sent to him. If the selected person accepts the appointment, the names of the others are put back on the list to be considered for future openings.

That is the rule in hiring from all kinds of eligible lists, whether they are for typist, carpenter, chemist, or something else. For every vacancy, the appointing officer has his choice of any one of the top three eligibles on the list. This explains why the person whose name is on top of the list sometimes does not get an appointment when some of the persons lower on the list do. If the appointing officer chooses the second or third eligible, the No. 1 eligible does not get a job at once, but stays on the list until he is appointed or the list is terminated.

X. HOW TO PASS THE INTERVIEW TEST

The examination for which you applied requires an oral interview test. You have already taken the written test and you are now being called for the interview test – the final part of the formal examination.

You may think that it is not possible to prepare for an interview test and that there are no procedures to follow during an interview. Our purpose is to point out some things you can do in advance that will help you and some good rules to follow and pitfalls to avoid while you are being interviewed.

What is an interview supposed to test?

The written examination is designed to test the technical knowledge and competence of the candidate; the oral is designed to evaluate intangible qualities, not readily measured otherwise, and to establish a list showing the relative fitness of each candidate – as measured against his competitors – for the position sought. Scoring is not on the basis of "right" and "wrong," but on a sliding scale of values ranging from "not passable" to "outstanding." As a matter of fact, it is possible to achieve a relatively low score without a single "incorrect" answer because of evident weakness in the qualities being measured.

Occasionally, an examination may consist entirely of an oral test – either an individual or a group oral. In such cases, information is sought concerning the technical knowledges and abilities of the candidate, since there has been no written examination for this purpose. More commonly, however, an oral test is used to supplement a written examination.

Who conducts interviews?

The composition of oral boards varies among different jurisdictions. In nearly all, a representative of the personnel department serves as chairman. One of the members of the board may be a representative of the department in which the candidate would work. In some cases, "outside experts" are used, and, frequently, a businessman or some other representative of the general public is asked to serve. Labor and management or other special groups may be represented. The aim is to secure the services of experts in the appropriate field.

However the board is composed, it is a good idea (and not at all improper or unethical) to ascertain in advance of the interview who the members are and what groups they represent. When you are introduced to them, you will have some idea of their backgrounds and interests, and at least you will not stutter and stammer over their names.

What should be done before the interview?

While knowledge about the board members is useful and takes some of the surprise element out of the interview, there is other preparation which is more substantive. It *is* possible to prepare for an oral interview – in several ways:

1) Keep a copy of your application and review it carefully before the interview

This may be the only document before the oral board, and the starting point of the interview. Know what education and experience you have listed there, and the sequence and dates of all of it. Sometimes the board will ask you to review the highlights of your experience for them; you should not have to hem and haw doing it.

2) Study the class specification and the examination announcement

Usually, the oral board has one or both of these to guide them. The qualities, characteristics or knowledges required by the position sought are stated in these documents. They offer valuable clues as to the nature of the oral interview. For example, if the job involves supervisory responsibilities, the announcement will usually indicate that knowledge of modern supervisory methods and the qualifications of the candidate as a supervisor will be tested. If so, you can expect such questions, frequently in the form of a hypothetical situation which you are expected to solve. NEVER go into an oral without knowledge of the duties and responsibilities of the job you seek.

3) Think through each qualification required

Try to visualize the kind of questions you would ask if you were a board member. How well could you answer them? Try especially to appraise your own knowledge and background in each area, *measured against the job sought*, and identify any areas in which you are weak. Be critical and realistic – do not flatter yourself.

4) Do some general reading in areas in which you feel you may be weak

For example, if the job involves supervision and your past experience has NOT, some general reading in supervisory methods and practices, particularly in the field of human relations, might be useful. Do NOT study agency procedures or detailed manuals. The oral board will be testing your understanding and capacity, not your memory.

5) Get a good night's sleep and watch your general health and mental attitude

You will want a clear head at the interview. Take care of a cold or any other minor ailment, and of course, no hangovers.

What should be done on the day of the interview?

Now comes the day of the interview itself. Give yourself plenty of time to get there. Plan to arrive somewhat ahead of the scheduled time, particularly if your appointment is in the fore part of the day. If a previous candidate fails to appear, the board might be ready for you a bit early. By early afternoon an oral board is almost invariably behind schedule if there are many candidates, and you may have to wait. Take along a book or magazine to read, or your application to review, but leave any extraneous material in the waiting room when you go in for your interview. In any event, relax and compose yourself.

The matter of dress is important. The board is forming impressions about you – from your experience, your manners, your attitude, and your appearance. Give your personal appearance careful attention. Dress your best, but not your flashiest. Choose conservative, appropriate clothing, and be sure it is immaculate. This is a business interview, and your appearance should indicate that you regard it as such. Besides, being well groomed and properly dressed will help boost your confidence.

Sooner or later, someone will call your name and escort you into the interview room. *This is it.* From here on you are on your own. It is too late for any more preparation. But remember, you asked for this opportunity to prove your fitness, and you are here because your request was granted.

What happens when you go in?

The usual sequence of events will be as follows: The clerk (who is often the board stenographer) will introduce you to the chairman of the oral board, who will introduce you to the other members of the board. Acknowledge the introductions before you sit down. Do not be surprised if you find a microphone facing you or a stenotypist sitting by. Oral interviews are usually recorded in the event of an appeal or other review.

Usually the chairman of the board will open the interview by reviewing the highlights of your education and work experience from your application – primarily for the benefit of the other members of the board, as well as to get the material into the record. Do not interrupt or comment unless there is an error or significant misinterpretation; if that is the case, do not hesitate. But do not quibble about insignificant matters. Also, he will usually ask you some question about your education, experience or your present job – partly to get you to start talking and to establish the interviewing "rapport." He may start the actual questioning, or turn it over to one of the other members. Frequently, each member undertakes the questioning on a particular area, one in which he is perhaps most competent, so you can expect each member to participate in the examination. Because time is limited, you may also expect some rather abrupt switches in the direction the questioning takes, so do not be upset by it. Normally, a board member will not pursue a single line of questioning unless he discovers a particular strength or weakness.

After each member has participated, the chairman will usually ask whether any member has any further questions, then will ask you if you have anything you wish to add. Unless you are expecting this question, it may floor you. Worse, it may start you off on an extended, extemporaneous speech. The board is not usually seeking more information. The question is principally to offer you a last opportunity to present further qualifications or to indicate that you have nothing to add. So, if you feel that a significant qualification or characteristic has been overlooked, it is proper to point it out in a sentence or so. Do not compliment the board on the thoroughness of their examination – they have been sketchy, and you know it. If you wish, merely say, "No thank you, I have nothing further to add." This is a point where you can "talk yourself out" of a good impression or fail to present an important bit of information. Remember, *you close the interview yourself.*

The chairman will then say, "That is all, Mr. _____, thank you." Do not be startled; the interview is over, and quicker than you think. Thank him, gather your belongings and take your leave. Save your sigh of relief for the other side of the door.

How to put your best foot forward

Throughout this entire process, you may feel that the board individually and collectively is trying to pierce your defenses, seek out your hidden weaknesses and embarrass and confuse you. Actually, this is not true. They are obliged to make an appraisal of your qualifications for the job you are seeking, and they want to see you in your best light. Remember, they must interview all candidates and a non-cooperative candidate may become a failure in spite of their best efforts to bring out his qualifications. Here are 15 suggestions that will help you:

1) Be natural – Keep your attitude confident, not cocky

If you are not confident that you can do the job, do not expect the board to be. Do not apologize for your weaknesses, try to bring out your strong points. The board is interested in a positive, not negative, presentation. Cockiness will antagonize any board member and make him wonder if you are covering up a weakness by a false show of strength.

2) Get comfortable, but don't lounge or sprawl

Sit erectly but not stiffly. A careless posture may lead the board to conclude that you are careless in other things, or at least that you are not impressed by the importance of the occasion. Either conclusion is natural, even if incorrect. Do not fuss with your clothing, a pencil or an ashtray. Your hands may occasionally be useful to emphasize a point; do not let them become a point of distraction.

3) Do not wisecrack or make small talk

This is a serious situation, and your attitude should show that you consider it as such. Further, the time of the board is limited – they do not want to waste it, and neither should you.

4) Do not exaggerate your experience or abilities

In the first place, from information in the application or other interviews and sources, the board may know more about you than you think. Secondly, you probably will not get away with it. An experienced board is rather adept at spotting such a situation, so do not take the chance.

5) If you know a board member, do not make a point of it, yet do not hide it

Certainly you are not fooling him, and probably not the other members of the board. Do not try to take advantage of your acquaintanceship – it will probably do you little good.

6) Do not dominate the interview

Let the board do that. They will give you the clues – do not assume that you have to do all the talking. Realize that the board has a number of questions to ask you, and do not try to take up all the interview time by showing off your extensive knowledge of the answer to the first one.

7) Be attentive

You only have 20 minutes or so, and you should keep your attention at its sharpest throughout. When a member is addressing a problem or question to you, give him your undivided attention. Address your reply principally to him, but do not exclude the other board members.

8) Do not interrupt

A board member may be stating a problem for you to analyze. He will ask you a question when the time comes. Let him state the problem, and wait for the question.

9) Make sure you understand the question

Do not try to answer until you are sure what the question is. If it is not clear, restate it in your own words or ask the board member to clarify it for you. However, do not haggle about minor elements.

10) Reply promptly but not hastily

A common entry on oral board rating sheets is "candidate responded readily," or "candidate hesitated in replies." Respond as promptly and quickly as you can, but do not jump to a hasty, ill-considered answer.

11) Do not be peremptory in your answers

A brief answer is proper – but do not fire your answer back. That is a losing game from your point of view. The board member can probably ask questions much faster than you can answer them.

12) Do not try to create the answer you think the board member wants

He is interested in what kind of mind you have and how it works – not in playing games. Furthermore, he can usually spot this practice and will actually grade you down on it.

13) Do not switch sides in your reply merely to agree with a board member

Frequently, a member will take a contrary position merely to draw you out and to see if you are willing and able to defend your point of view. Do not start a debate, yet do not surrender a good position. If a position is worth taking, it is worth defending.

14) Do not be afraid to admit an error in judgment if you are shown to be wrong

The board knows that you are forced to reply without any opportunity for careful consideration. Your answer may be demonstrably wrong. If so, admit it and get on with the interview.

15) Do not dwell at length on your present job

The opening question may relate to your present assignment. Answer the question but do not go into an extended discussion. You are being examined for a *new* job, not your present one. As a matter of fact, try to phrase ALL your answers in terms of the job for which you are being examined.

Basis of Rating

Probably you will forget most of these "do's" and "don'ts" when you walk into the oral interview room. Even remembering them all will not ensure you a passing grade. Perhaps you did not have the qualifications in the first place. But remembering them will help you to put your best foot forward, without treading on the toes of the board members.

Rumor and popular opinion to the contrary notwithstanding, an oral board wants you to make the best appearance possible. They know you are under pressure – but they also want to see how you respond to it as a guide to what your reaction would be under the pressures of the job you seek. They will be influenced by the degree of poise you display, the personal traits you show and the manner in which you respond.

ABOUT THIS BOOK

This book contains tests divided into Examination Sections. Go through each test, answering every question in the margin. We have also attached a sample answer sheet at the back of the book that can be removed and used. At the end of each test look at the answer key and check your answers. On the ones you got wrong, look at the right answer choice and learn. Do not fill in the answers first. Do not memorize the questions and answers, but understand the answer and principles involved. On your test, the questions will likely be different from the samples. Questions are changed and new ones added. If you understand these past questions you should have success with any changes that arise. Tests may consist of several types of questions. We have additional books on each subject should more study be advisable or necessary for you. Finally, the more you study, the better prepared you will be. This book is intended to be the last thing you study before you walk into the examination room. Prior study of relevant texts is also recommended. NLC publishes some of these in our Fundamental Series. Knowledge and good sense are important factors in passing your exam. Good luck also helps. So now study this Passbook, absorb the material contained within and take that knowledge into the examination. Then do your best to pass that exam.

EXAMINATION SECTION

EXAMINATION SECTION
TEST 1

DIRECTION: Each question or incomplete statement is followed by several suggested answers or completions. Select the one the BEST answers the question or completes the statement. *PRINT THE LETTER OF THE CORRECT ANSWER IN THE SPACE AT THE RIGHT.*

1. Most state child support enforcement (CSE) offices review support orders every _____ if the family is receiving federal assistance/ TANF.

    A. 6 months
    B. 1 year
    C. 3 years
    D. 5 years

    1._____

2. A mother claims that the father of her child is unknown to her. The child support enforcement agency conducts multiple interviews with her, and requires her to complete paternity paperwork several times. The intent of this approach is usually to

    A. compel the remembrance of a forgotten event
    B. protect the agency and the investigator against liability
    C. reveal inconsistencies and penetrate false stories
    D. elicit financial data that can be passed on to public assistance agencies

    2._____

3. The Federal Parent Locator Service (FPLS) can search for a person's current address in the records of each of the data sources, EXCEPT the

    A. Internal Revenue Service (IRS)
    B. Bureau of the Census
    C. National Directory of New Hires (NDNH)
    D. Department of Veterans Affairs

    3._____

4. The allocation of child support collected to the various types of debt within a support case (monthly support obligations, arrears, ordered arrears, etc.) is known as

    A. offset
    B. distribution
    C. imputation
    D. wage assignment

    4._____

5. A child who is the subject of a support order reaches the legal age of emancipation. Typically, the noncustodial parent is

    A. still required to pay any outstanding arrearage, plus interest, and any attachment liens, or other enforcement options are still in effect
    B. still required to pay any outstanding arrearage, plus interest,
    C. no longer liable for any portion of an outstanding child support debt
    D. required to pay only the principle of any existing arrearage

    5._____

6. A caseworker reviews a mother's application for child support enforcement, but finds that the application contains very little useful information. The child was born out of wedlock. Typically, the caseworker's next step is to

   A. conduct a paternity interview
   B. obtain photographs of the potential fathers from the department of motor vehicles
   C. consult FPLS or a state parent locator service
   D. open a case file for the mother and make a record of the mother's actions thus far

7. In child support enforcement cases, paternity is legally and irreversibly established by
   I. the appearance of the father's name on the birth certificate
   II. voluntary stipulation
   III. a default judgement
   IV. a blood test

   A. I or IV
   B. II, III or IV
   C. II or IV
   D. IV only

8. In most states' child support formulas, net pay is determined by deducting each of the following from gross wages, EXCEPT

   A. health insurance premiums
   B. 401(k) plan contributions
   C. state and federal taxes
   D. union dues

9. What is the term for the practice by which one state or country voluntarily recognizes the judgements or decisions of another?

   A. Extradition
   B. Comity
   C. Pro se
   D. Arrearages

10. The most common tool used to collect child support payments that are not voluntarily made is through

    A. a lien
    B. tax refund intercept
    C. civil contempt of court proceedings
    D. wage assignment

11. The federal government has established time schedules in which all child support enforcement agencies must perform certain actions. Within five days, an agency is required to

    A. open a new case after application or referral
    B. take action after verifying new information on the location of the noncustodial parent
    C. check the records of local, state, and federal resources if the noncustodial parent has disappeared
    D. reserve an existing wage assignment after employment verification

12. Through the *long-arm* service that allows caseworkers to reach noncustodial parents anywhere in the United States, a summons and complaint is first served to the noncustodial parent by means of   12._____

    A. the child support enforcement agency for the jurisdiction where the noncustodial parent resides
    B. certified mail
    C. the law enforcement agency for the jurisdiction in which the noncustodial parent resides
    D. an agent of the United States Justice Department, typically FBI

13. The IRS full collection process can be used only for cases in which the amount owed is at least $_____.   13._____

    A. 500
    B. 750
    C. 1500
    D. 3000

14. Typically, a maximum of_____% of the income that a noncustodial parent receives from pension or retirement benefits can be garnished for purposes of child support.   14._____

    A. 10
    B. 25
    C. 35
    D. 50

15. Under the terms of the Uniform Interstate Family Support Act (UIFSA), a noncustodial parent may contest the validity or enforcement of a wage assignment order received from another state. Viable claims that may defeat the service of a wage assignment include   15._____

    I. modification of the child support order by a court in the state where the noncustodial parent lives
    II. an error in the calculation of the current amount owed
    III. the person on whose employer the wage assignment was served is not the obligor named in the underlying child support order
    IV. death of the child for whose benefit the wage assignment was served

    A. I and IV
    B. II, III and IV
    C. III and IV
    D. I, II, III and IV

16. What is the term for a court order directing a person to appear and present any evidence as to why the remedies stated in a child support order should not be confirmed or executed?   16._____

    A. Writ of execution
    B. Attachment
    C. Show cause
    D. Estoppel

17. For all initial orders which are not established through the Child Support Enforcement program, wage withholding on the obligor occurs

    A. as soon as a payment is late for any reason
    B. if there is an arrearage of at least $1000
    C. if there is an arrearage in the amount of at least one month's obligation
    D. immediately

18. Which of the following types of accounts are NOT typically subject to the federal financial institution data match (FDIM) program?

    A. Demand deposit accounts
    B. Mutual funds
    C. Pension funds
    D. Time deposit accounts

19. An *ex parte* wage assignment

    A. does not pertain to arrearages owed by noncustodial parents
    B. may order that more than 50 percent of a noncustodial parent's wages be withheld and sent to the child support enforcement agency each month
    C. is obtained by compulsion, without notice and without the cooperation of the non-paying noncustodial parent
    D. is an administrative, rather than a judicial process

20. A noncustodial parent receives a summons and complaint in a child support enforcement action. The parent's answer to the complaint is legally valid if it is
    I. telephoned in to the child support enforcement agency
    II. filed with the clerk of the court for the jurisdiction where the noncustodial parent resides, if it is a different jurisdiction than the custodial parent's
    III. filed with the clerk of the court that issued the summons
    IV. filed with the child support enforcement agency that requested the summons

    A. I or IV
    B. I, III or IV
    C. III only
    D. I, II, III or IV

21. When a noncustodial parent is more than _____ delinquent in her or his child support obligation, the child support enforcement agency is required by law to submit the parent's name, the amount owed, and the payment history on the arrearage to credit reporting agencies.

    A. 30 days
    B. 2 months
    C. 6 months
    D. 1 year

22. Which of the following is a function of the federal administrative offset program?   22._____

    A. Denial of passport issuance by the Secretary of State to an obligor with an above-threshold debt
    B. Offsetting federal tax refunds owed to obligors
    C. Identification of accounts located in multistate financial institutions held by delinquent obligors
    D. Offsetting payments from federal agencies (payments due private vendors, federal retirement benefits, travel reimbursements)

23. A civil money judgement may be enforced by the seizure of a debtor's real or personal property. This action is known as   23._____

    A. a lien
    B. execution
    C. garnishment
    D. estoppel

24. In order to tap assets such as bank accounts, funds held in vacation or trust accounts, and property that the noncustodial parent stands to inherit, the most commonly used tool by child support enforcement agencies is the   24._____

    A. property lien
    B. state/federal tax intercept
    C. writ of execution
    D. bankruptcy law

25. Under the Welfare Reform Act,   25._____

    A. financial institutions are held liable for revealing the Social Security numbers of noncustodial parents who maintain accounts and owe past-due child support
    B. financial institutions are required by federal law to provide the names, addresses, and other identifying information on all noncustodial parents who maintain accounts and owe past-due child support
    C. financial institutions are held liable for honoring the levy or writ of execution on a parent's bank account
    D. the financial institution data-match (FIDM) process is established as an entity that falls under federal authority and administration

26. A custodial parent has failed to keep good financial records, including copies of past tax returns. A local search for a non-custodial spouse's social security number turns up nothing. The most useful next step in the investigation would be to determine whether   26._____

    A. the non-custodial parent's name is on any old insurance policies
    B. the parents filed a joint income tax return in the last three years
    C. the non-custodial parent was ever a patient at any nearby hospitals
    D. past employers might have the number

27. The IRS may enforce full collection for delinquent child support payments by levying against income and assets, which may include   27._____

    A. workmen's compensation
    B. tax refunds
    C. undelivered mail
    D. wearing apparel

28. Some sources of income are subject to automatic withholding pursuant to state law and do not require a wage assignment. These income sources typically include the following, EXCEPT

    A. state disability insurance benefits
    B. worker's compensation benefits
    C. unemployment insurance benefits
    D. lottery winnings

29. A noncustodial parent is incarcerated, and assumes that no action is needed to modify an exiting child support order. This parent should know that

    A. arrearages due upon the date of his incarceration will remain the same, but he will not be liable for interest that accumulates while he is incarcerated
    B. the garnishment of wages from all future employment will probably be set at 25 percent
    C. without a modifying court order, the arrearages will accumulate at the same rate and cannot be discharged
    D. he will need to find some source of income while incarcerated to maintain the current level of support

30. The portion of the Social Security Act covering the federal child support enforcement program is Title

    A. IV-A
    B. IV-D
    C. IV-E
    D. V-A

31. When a noncustodial parent who owes child support arrearages files for Chapter 7 bankruptcy,

    A. the noncustodial parent is seeking to set up a workable payment plan in which creditors—including the child support enforcement agency—each receive a portion of his or her assets
    B. child support enforcement agencies are required to file a petition with the bankruptcy court in order to protect against the discharge of child support arrearages
    C. child support enforcement agencies must stop their efforts to collect child support arrearages that accrued prior to the date the noncustodial parent filed, until the bankruptcy has been discharged
    D. the court refuses to discharge the bankruptcy claim until after the arrearages are paid

32. Which of the following is NOT a provision of the Uniform Interstate Family Support Act (UIFSA)?

    A. states are required by law to enforce against their own residents the orders made by others states
    B. employers are subject to the jurisdiction of child support orders entered in other states, even if the employers do not do business in the states that enter the support orders
    C. only one court order will exist for the support of a child, no matter how often or where the parents and child move
    D. out-of-state orders must be registered in the state where the noncustodial parent lives

33. Blood tests used to establish paternity are typically paid for by the noncustodial parent
     I. when the noncustodial parent does not receive public assistance
     II. when the test establishes paternity
     III. in most cases

    A. I only
    B. I and II
    C. II only
    D. III only

34. To which of the following items of property could a lien be attached for the purpose of enforcing child support?

    A. A moving van used in a business owned by the parent
    B. The parent's personal vehicle
    C. Acreage farmed by the parent
    D. A primary residence

35. An order for monthly child support was $150 per month, effective October 1, 1985. A compounding interest rate of 10 percent applies to arrearages. The only child support ever paid by this parent was received through tax refund intercepts. When the case was audited on December 31, 2006, the total balance owed by this parent, including principal and interest, would have been approximately

    A. $5,800
    B. $640
    C. $12,800
    D. $24,000

36. A child support enforcement agency receives an application from a custodial mother, who claims that the child's father is a military officer who lives on a military base. The summons and complaint can be issued

    A. through the Office of the Judge Advocate General
    B. by a process server granted access to the base
    C. by certified mail
    D. through the court with jurisdiction in the adjacent civilian sector

37. A major consideration in screening a case for federal prosecution under the Child Support Recovery Act of 1992 is whether all reasonably available civil and state criminal remedies have been pursued first. Next, priority is given to each of the following cases, EXCEPT where

    A. failure to make support payments is connected to some other federal offense such as bankruptcy fraud.
    B. there is a pattern of moving from State to State to avoid payment
    C. the parent is receiving cash assistance from either the state or federal government
    D. there is a pattern of deception (e.g., use of false name or social security number)

38. Which of the following is NOT a common feature between the federal OCSE-conducted data match program with multistate financial institutions (MSFIDM) and the process for financial institutions using the single-state process (SSFIDM)?

    A. Match methods (all accounts/matched accounts) used
    B. Frequency of match conduct
    C. Types of accounts matched
    D. Participating institutions

39. A caseworker files a UIFSA petition for paternity. Under federal guidelines, the CSE office in the initiating state is required to provide the court with the information it needs within

    A. 7 days
    B. 30 days
    C. 90 days
    D. 1 year

40. The IRS full collection process can be used only for cases in which the past-due obligation is equal to at least _____ worth of monthly payments.

    A. one month's
    B. three months'
    C. six months'
    D. one year's

KEY (CORRECT ANSWERS)

1. C	11. D	21. B	31. C
2. C	12. B	22. D	32. D
3. B	13. B	23. B	33. C
4. B	14. B	24. C	34. B
5. A	15. B	25. B	35. D
6. A	16. C	26. B	36. A
7. D	17. D	27. B	37. C
8. B	18. C	28. B	38. A
9. B	19. C	29. C	39. B
10. D	20. C	30. B	40. B

TEST 2

DIRECTIONS: Each question or incomplete statement is followed by several suggested answers or completions. Select the one the BEST answers the question or completes the statement. *PRINT THE LETTER OF THE CORRECT ANSWER IN THE SPACE AT THE RIGHT.*

1. To find the current address of a noncustodial parent, a child support enforcement caseworker consults the parent's former employer. The most likely reason for the employer's having the parent's current address is a

    A. legal requirement to mail a W-2 form to the former employee
    B. friendship between the parent and former employer
    C. possibility that the parent still works for the employer
    D. possibility that other employees at the workplace may know where the parent is

1.____

2. The father of a child has told the mother that she will never get a paternity judgement on him, because he will simply leave the state. The mother's only remedy is to

    A. compel paternity testing of the father
    B. seek voluntary support payments
    C. resort to abnormal specimen testing
    D. seek a default paternity judgement

2.____

3. A noncustodial parent owes substantial child support arrearages. The child support enforcement caseworker suggests locating the noncustodial parent's bank accounts, and says he'll need the name of the bank, the branch location, and the account numbers. The noncustodial parent has refused to supply this information. The simplest source for this information is the

    A. last check written by the noncustodial parent
    B. FPLS
    C. noncustodial parent's employer
    D. financial institution data-match (FIDM) process

3.____

4. Which of the following is a legal means of abating, reducing or increasing a court order for child support?

    A. A court order that modifies the first one
    B. The incarceration of the noncustodial parent
    C. A change in the financial circumstances of the noncustodial parent
    D. A *reserve* order

4.____

5. Under federal bankruptcy laws,

    A. no portion of a child support-related obligation may be deferred through a recognized claim of bankruptcy
    B. child support reimbursement owed on welfare cases may be discharged through a recognized claim of bankruptcy
    C. child support enforcement agencies are required to file a petition with the noncustodial parent's bankruptcy court in order to protect against the discharge of child support arrearages
    D. no portion of any child support-related debt is dischargeable through a recognized claim of bankruptcy

5.____

6. A custodial mother requests that a review be conducted for possible upward modification of a support order, and has submitted income and expense declaration forms to the child support enforcement agency. The noncustodial father, not anxious for the review process to begin, delays the completion of his own declarations. The father should know that

   A. this is a good opportunity to file a counter-request for considering downward modification
   B. after a period of 30 days, the review process can and will proceed without his input
   C. any modifications that occur will be retroactive to the date the request was filed
   D. the review cannot take place until he has complied with the agency's request for information

7. What is the term for the amount of money taken from a parent's state or federal income tax refund to satisfy a child support debt?

   A. Lien
   B. Garnishment
   C. Obligor
   D. Offset

8. Other than parents' respective net income and assets, the most significant factor in calculating the amount of guideline child support to be paid by the noncustodial parent will be

   A. special circumstances such as medical expenses
   B. time spent with the child
   C. the Rothbarth marginal cost estimation
   D. the number of children in common between parents

9. The requirement that courts must recognize and enforce an order that has been validly entered by another court is known as

   A. full faith and credit
   B. bench warrant
   C. comity
   D. obligation

10. A custodial parent lives with a child in New York, the state that issued an existing child support order. The noncustodial parent lives in Ohio. A few years after the order is issued, the custodial parent and child move to Florida. Under the terms of the Uniform Interstate Family Support Act (UIFSA), which of the following is true?

    A. The New York support order follows the custodial parent and child to Florida, but New York no longer has continuing exclusive authority over the support order.
    B. There is no controlling authority for the terms of the support order.
    C. Exclusive authority over the support order is transported to Florida.
    D. The state of Ohio, where the noncustodial parent lives, is granted limited authority to modify the existing support order.

11. By means of certified mail, a caseworker sends a summons and complaint to a noncustodial parent who resides in another state. The letter is returned unsigned. The caseworker's next step should be to

    A. notify the federal Office of Child Support Enforcement
    B. deliver the documents to the county sheriff in the jurisdiction where the noncustodial parent resides
    C. send a *notice of intent to close case* letter to the custodial parent
    D. deliver the documents by hand to the noncustodial parent

12. In child support enforcement cases, paternity is legally established by
    I. the appearance of the father's name on the birth certificate
    II. voluntary stipulation
    III. a default judgement
    IV. a blood test

    A. I or IV
    B. II or IV
    C. II, III or IV
    D. I, II, III or IV

13. Under the terms of the federal financial institution data match (FDIM) program, states are required to develop and operate a system in which financial institutions provide the name, address, and other identifying information for each non-custodial parent who maintains an account at the institution and who owes past-due support. By law, this information is to be provided and updated

    A. monthly
    B. quarterly
    C. bimonthly
    D. annually

14. A caseworker's investigation strongly suggests that a significant real estate asset, nominally in the possession of a third party, is actually owned by a non-custodial parent. To prove that the non-custodial parent is the owner of this property, the custodial parent must file a(n)

    A. escheatment
    B. quitclaim
    C. estoppel
    D. creditor's bill

15. When a noncustodial parent who owes child support arrearages files for Chapter 13 bankruptcy,
    I. the child support enforcement agency must wait 90 days from the filing of the petition before resuming collection procedures on arrearages
    II. support arrearages that occurred before the filing of the petition are subject to the terms of the bankruptcy plan
    III. any tax refunds intercepted by the child support enforcement agency after they have been listed in the bankruptcy plan must be turned over to the trustee
    IV. the child support enforcement agency may not enforce a wage assignment on current child support payments

A. I only
B. I, II and III
C. II and III
D. I, II, III and IV

16. States can request an offset of Federal income tax refunds for past-due support of over $_____ on behalf of minor children not receiving cash assistance (TANF), as well as over $_____ owed to States that have provided assistance.

    A. 500; 150
    B. 1000; 750
    C. 2000; 1500
    D. 5000; 3000

17. Noncustodial fathers are typically allowed _____ to rescind a voluntary paternity declaration if a mistake has been made, and, if fraud, a material error, or duress is established, _____.

    A. 30 days; an additional year
    B. 60 days; an additional year
    C. 90 days; an additional two years
    D. 90 days; an indefinite period of time

18. In order to prosecute under this Child Support Recovery Act of 1992, the United States Attorney's Office must prove that the noncustodial parent was financially able to meet his/her obligation at the time the payment was due. If support arrearages are more than $_____ or are unpaid for longer than _____, the noncustodial parent is subject to punishment.

    A. 1,000; 6 months
    B. 2,500; 1 year
    C. 5,000; 1 year
    D. 10,000; 6 months

19. A child is being raised by foster parents, and the case is deferred to the child support enforcement agency for defray the costs of foster care. In terms of the Social Security Act, this is known as a _____ case.

    A. IV-A
    B. IV-D
    C. IV-E
    D. non-IV-D

20. A custodial father tells a caseworker that he suspects his child's mother is still in the area, though he can't find her. The most important items of information necessary for finding the mother will be

    A. addresses and phone numbers of relatives and friends
    B. names of unions, clubs, or organizations to which she might belong
    C. information about local creditors such as banks or utilities
    D. her social security number and current employer's name

21. When a *reserved* child support order is issued, this means that
    A. the noncustodial parent will not have to pay back child support for a period during which he or she had no income
    B. support payments must include reimbursements for federal aid (TANF) received by the custodial parent
    C. the court cannot make the support order retroactive
    D. the amount of support will be established at a later date

22. The federal financial institution data match (FDIM) program
    I. is available only in case situations where there is an existing arrearage
    II. is often used as a locate tool in paternity adjudication
    III. can be used for collections or payment enforcement
    IV. can be used to modify an existing support order

    A. I only
    B. I and II
    C. I, III and IV
    D. I, II, III and IV

23. Assuming no arrearages, the amount that can be withheld from an employee's disposable wages is limited by the Federal Consumer Credit Protection Act (FCCPA) to_____% of disposable earnings if the obligated parent has a second family, and_____% if there is no second family.

    A. 25; 50
    B. 35; 50
    C. 50; 60
    D. 65; 75

24. Which of the following forms of income does NOT typically require a wage assignment for the purpose of automatic withholding?
    A. Unemployment insurance benefits
    B. Severance pay
    C. Social security retirement benefits
    D. Commissions

25. The amount of time a CSE Office can try to collect on a child support debt is primarily determined by
    A. the current circumstances of the custodial parent
    B. the age of the youngest child included in the support agreement
    C. the current circumstances of the non-custodial parent
    D. state statutes of limitations

26. A child support enforcement caseworker, suspicious of a noncustodial parent's new luxurious lifestyle, investigates and discovers that the parent has recently won the state lottery. In most states,_____% of lottery winnings are subject to be intercepted and paid in the form of child support

    A. 10   B. 25
    C. 50   D. 100

27. Intact family cases

    A. are usually referred to the child support enforcement agency by the welfare department
    B. typically involve missing noncustodial parents
    C. are not within the jurisdiction of child support enforcement agencies
    D. have different support order requirements

28. In a child support enforcement case, a noncustodial parent received fringe benefits from an employer that may be taxable, but cannot be counted as additional disposable income that is subject to child support obligations. This income is described as

    A. frozen
    B. alleged
    C. nonreviewable
    D. imputed

29. Searches of state and federal tax returns, current and past employers, bank records, insurance policies, credit cards, payslips, and even local hospitals have failed to reveal the social security number of the non-custodial parent. The caseworker can still find the social security number, if he or she has at least three important pieces of information. Which of the following is NOT one of them?

    A. Date of birth
    B. Mother's maiden name
    C. Place of birth
    D. Ethnic census category

30. If a child support enforcement agency needs to file a property lien to collect arrearages from a noncustodial parent, it is imperative that

    A. the lien be filed before the moneys are paid to the noncustodial parent
    B. the amount of the property sale or settlement does not exceed the amount of the lien
    C. the lien be placed on real property, rather than a civil judgement or worker's compensation settlement
    D. if the lien is drawn for real estate, there are no other existing liens on the property

31. Under federal confidentiality provisions, a child support enforcement agency that receives information from the IRS on a taxpayer's return or filing status must submit a Safeguard Procedures Report at least _____ days before the scheduled receipt of the information.

    A. 7
    B. 10
    C. 30
    D. 45

32. The federal government has established time schedules in which all child support enforcement agencies must perform certain actions. Within ninety days, an agency is required to

    A. respond to a request from another jurisdiction for information
    B. respond to a parent's written request for information
    C. establish a support order or complete service of process after locating a noncustodial parent and/or establishing paternity
    D. initiate interstate action upon verifying that the noncustodial parent is in another state or jurisdiction

33. When using the FPLS to find a noncustodial parent, a child support enforcement caseworker should
    I. remember that IRS information is most current in July
    II. make sure that the project coordinator and safeguard official are different people, to protect the confidentiality of IRS information
    III. remember that IRS information may be used in litigation against a non-custodial parent
    IV. make an OCSE-HHS application for address information before turning to a state PLS

    A. I only
    B. I and II
    C. II and III
    D. I, II, III and IV

34. A child support enforcement agency issues a summons and complaint to an alleged father who is on active duty as a member of the armed services. The defendant does not file an Answer for paternity or child support. The caseworker's next step should be to

    A. conduct a paternity interview with the custodial mother
    B. request a default judgement against the defendant
    C. notify the Office of the Judge Advocate General
    D. request that that court appoint an attorney to represent the absent defendant

35. Approximately_____% of all child support cases in the United States are interstate cases; a little less than_____% of nationwide child support collections are from interstate cases.

    A. 10; 20
    B. 20; 15
    C. 33; 10
    D. 50; 33

36. A noncustodial parent claims a hardship deduction to reduce the amount of income used to formulate child support. Allowable reasons for applying a hardship deduction include
    I. the support of a family member who has a life-threatening illness
    II. a personal illness that creates financial hardship
    III. the support of a live-in dependent parent
    IV. the payment of a large and burdensome mortgage

    A. I and II
    B. I, II and III
    C. II only
    D. I, II, III and IV

37. A child support enforcement caseworker requests a noncustodial parent's current address from the IRS's Individual Master File (IMF). Typically, the caseworker can expect to receive a reply in about

    A. 5 days
    B. 10 days
    C. 3 weeks
    D. 6 weeks

38. Child support enforcement agencies are required to report to the welfare department any fraud they uncover in investigations. Most of these referrals involve

    A. appointed legal guardians
    B. live-in noncustodial parents
    C. multiple social security numbers for dependent children
    D. foster parents

39. Under the Uniform Interstate Family Support Act (UIFSA), a state that initiates a child support order can usually apply the *long arm* jurisdiction over a nonresident noncustodial parent when the
    I. child was conceived in the initiating state as a result of intercourse between the noncustodial parent and custodial parent
    II. noncustodial parent files an answer to a child support petition
    III. noncustodial parent lived in the initiating state and provided prenatal expenses or support for the child
    IV. child lived in the initiating state with the noncustodial parent

    A. I only
    B. I and IV
    C. II, III and IV
    D. I, II, III and IV

40. Applications that are submitted by a child support enforcement agency for an IRS full collection must include each of the following, EXCEPT

    A. the noncustodial parent's current address and place of employment
    B. the court order number and date
    C. a summary of the collection actions taken in the case and the reasons why specific collection actions by the state's child support enforcement program have not been used or been effective
    D. the names and social security numbers of the children who are owed child support

KEY (CORRECT ANSWERS)

1.	A	11.	B	21.	D	31.	D
2.	D	12.	C	22.	C	32.	C
3.	A	13.	B	23.	C	33.	A
4.	A	14.	D	24.	A	34.	D
5.	D	15.	B	25.	D	35.	C
6.	B	16.	A	26.	D	36.	B
7.	D	17.	B	27.	A	37.	C
8.	B	18.	C	28.	D	38.	B
9.	A	19.	C	29.	D	39.	D
10.	A	20.	D	30.	A	40.	A

EXAMINATION SECTION
TEST 1

DIRECTIONS: Each question or incomplete statement is followed by several suggested answers or completions. Select the one that BEST answers the question or completes the statement. *PRINT THE LETTER OF THE CORRECT ANSWER IN THE SPACE AT THE RIGHT.*

1. Local responsibility for the relief of economic need long having been recognized as inadequate, the state and federal governments have established schemes of *categorical* assistance and social insurance.
   In the preceding sentence, the italicized word means MOST NEARLY
   A. conditional   B. economic   C. pecuniary   D. classified

   1._____

2. When a person *vicariously* lives out his own problems in novels and plays, he is engaging in an experience that is, in terms of the italicized word in this sentence
   A. dynamic   B. monastic   C. substituted   D. dignified

   2._____

3. The Alcoholics Anonymous program, which in essence amounts to a *therapeutic* procedure, is codified into twelve steps.
   The italicized word in the preceding sentence means MOST NEARLY
   A. compensatory   B. curative   C. sequential   D. volitional

   3._____

4. The case of Mary Smith who ordered her husband out of the house and begged his pardon before he could leave, if accepted as characteristic behavior on the part of this woman, is BEST considered as an illustration of
   A. ambivalence   B. compensation
   C. retrogression   D. frustration

   4._____

5. To say that the Community Chest movement seems to have been *indigenous* to the North American continent describes this movement, in terms of the italicized word in this sentence MOST NEARLY as
   A. imported   B. essential   C. native   D. homogeneous

   5._____

6. There should be no *opprobrium* attached to the term "second-hand housing" since every house is second-hand after the first occupancy.
   The italicized word in the preceding sentence means MOST NEARLY
   A. stigma   B. honor   C. rank   D. credit

   6._____

7. Clinics are now seeing many people who complain of seriously disturbed feelings and other symptoms relating to *traumatic* war experiences.
   In the preceding sentence, the italicized word means MOST NEARLY
   A. recent   B. worldwide   C. prodigious   D. shocking

   7._____

8. The nature of the *pathology* underlying the compulsion is obscure.
   In the preceding sentence, the italicized word means MOST NEARLY
   A. drive B. disease C. deterioration D. development

9. If the interests of a social welfare agency are concerned with bringing opportunities for self-help to underprivileged *ethnic* groups, its activities involve MOST NEARLY, in terms of the italicized word in this sentence,
   A. racial factors
   B. minority units
   C. religious affiliations
   D. economic conditions

10. Increased facilities for medical care (though interrupted to some extent by the *exigencies* of wartime) will safeguard the health of many children who in previous generations would have been doomed to an early death or to physical disability.
    In the above sentence the MOST NEARLY CORRECT equivalent of the italicized word is
    A. obstacles B. occurrences C. extenuations D. exactions

11. The name of Sanford Bate would be associated by a well-read social service worker with the book entitled
    A. THE FAMILY
    B. SOCIAL CHANGE
    C. PRISONS AND BEYOND
    D. HULL HOUSE

Questions 12-16.

DIRECTIONS: In Questions 12 through 16 below, Column I consists of items referring to certain characteristics of areas usually found to exist in most American cities. Column II describes four sections into which the general sociological pattern of the modern city may be divided. Select the description in Column II to which the reference in Column I is MOST appropriate.

COLUMN I

12. The area in which a predominantly male resident population would probably be found.

13. The area in which a *slum* would probably be located if it existed in this city.

14. The area in which the most prominent citizens of the community would probably be found living

15. The area likely to contain the sparsest resident population

16. The area likely to be inhabited by middle-class families

COLUMN II

A. Retail stores, eating establishments, motion picture theater, offices of professional people and business organizations
B. Made-over private dwellings, rooming houses, cheap hotels pawnbrokers, wholesale business establishments
C. Less crowding than in above area, more modern houses, fewer children, wives not generally gainfully employed
D. Fashionable suburbs homes of professional and business leaders, relative cleanliness and modernity

3 (#1)

17. To the social service worker who has maintained an interest in the field of psychiatry, THE NEUROTIC PERSONALITY OF OUR TIME would suggest
    A. Margaret Mead
    B. R.S. Lynd and H.M. Lynd
    C. Karen Horney
    D. Ruth Benedict

17.____

18. The conscientious social service worker is interested in the provisions of the Wagner-Ellender-Taft bill because the subject of this Congressional legislation was
    A. rent control
    B. housing
    C. tax reduction
    D. health insurance

18.____

19. Of the following, the name MOST closely identified with developments leading to the enactment of the Social Security Act was
    A. Harry Hopkins
    B. William Beveridge
    C. Herbert C. Hoover
    D. Arthur J. Altmeyer

19.____

20. The federal government will grant reimbursement under the Social Security Act to states for certain categories of assistance, provided the state law is in conformance with the requirements of the Act.
    One of the following requirements which is enforced by the federal government is that
    A. citizenship must be required as a condition of eligibility
    B. some residence requirement must be included
    C. payment to the client must be *money payment*
    D. some exemptions from merit system operation must be provided

20.____

21. Of the following social services administered by public agencies, the one administered by the federal government is
    A. unemployment compensation
    B. old age and survivors insurance
    C. vocational rehabilitation for civilians
    D. civilian war assistance

21.____

22. Most old age assistance program have been limited in general to the financial and physical needs of the aged because
    A. it is impossible to determine their other needs with any degree of practicality
    B. social agencies are unwilling to enlarge their responsibilities for the care of the aged
    C. old people are not interested in social participation
    D. public relief administrators have not been given the means to undertake more augmented programs

22.____

23. Of the qualifications and procedures connected with the method under which an insured individual may receive old age and survivors insurance, three are given below.

23.____

The statement which is NOT among these qualifications or procedures is that the individual
- A. must have been employed in covered employment for certain specified periods of time
- B. must have attained the age of 65
- C. has his primary benefit amounts computed in relation to his record earnings in covered employment
- D. is disqualified to receive old-age and survivors insurance benefits for any month in which he had an earned income of $100 or less

24. One of the requirements regarding an institution in which the Department of Social Service may place a neglected child is that the institution must
    - A. have been certified by the State Board of Social Welfare
    - B. be operated on a non-sectarian basis
    - C. have been incorporated for a period of not less than three years
    - D. be situated within the geographical limits of the city

25. With respect to destitute children placed out in institutions as public charges, the Commissioner of Social Services
    - A. may not deputize subordinates to make an investigation of such an institution except through the Department of Licenses
    - B. may reimburse such an institution for any expense, other than salaries, actually incurred in the placing out
    - C. may not authorize an institution to which a child has been committed to place such a child in a family
    - D. may transfer a child from one institution to another, except when either institution is governed by persons professing the same religious faith as the parents of the child

26. George Bailey, who has been unable to earn a living because of a recent industrial accident, is referred to his nearest social services center and subsequently placed in an institution for rehabilitation and training so that he will become a permanent charge upon the public. Bailey has a son whom the social service reports as unwilling, though sufficiently able, to support his incapacitated father.
    If the Commissioner of Social Services wishes to compel Bailey's son to pay a reasonable charge for Bailey's care in the institution, he would apply for the necessary order to the
    - A. Family Court
    - B. Supreme Court
    - C. State Board of Social Services
    - D. Court of Appeals

27. Commitment by the Department of Social Services invariably implies that the parents
    - A. have maltreated the child
    - B. are unable to support the child
    - C. have, through voluntary agreement, given custody of the child to the Commissioner of Social Services
    - D. have given the child up for adoption

28. The service of the Department of Social Services which is financed jointly by the city, state, and federal governments is
    A. veterans assistance
    B. aid to dependent children
    C. home relief
    D. the cost of board in foster home care for children

29. The LEAST applicable of the following statements regarding unemployment compensation for workers in this state is
    A. the employer pays the total tax for unemployment compensation
    B. the maximum period of benefit payments is 26 weeks in any benefit year
    C. benefit payments are the same whether a person has been discharged from his job on account of retrenchment or is unemployed on account of illness
    D. employees of philanthropic and religious organizations are not included in coverage

30. Ten months ago, Mr. Johnson came to this city from Plattsburgh, New York, where he had lived for ten years. Unable to find work, he applies at your welfare center for assistance for himself and his family.
    As an acting intake interviewer, you should tell Mr. Johnson that
    A. he is ineligible for relief since his needs are the responsibility of another municipality
    B. he is ineligible for relief and should return to Plattsburgh because no jobs are available in this city
    C. he should wait two more months in order to attain the required year's settlement
    D. his application is acceptable and his eligibility on the basis of need will be determined

KEY (CORRECT ANSWERS)

1.	D	11.	C	21.	B
2.	C	12.	B	22.	D
3.	B	13.	B	23.	D
4.	A	14.	D	24.	A
5.	C	15.	A	25.	B
6.	A	16.	C	26.	A
7.	D	17.	C	27.	C
8.	B	18.	B	28.	B
9.	A	19.	A	29.	C
10.	D	20.	C	30.	D

TEST 2

DIRECTIONS: Each question or incomplete statement is followed by several suggested answers or completions. Select the one that BEST answers the question or completes the statement. *PRINT THE LETTER OF THE CORRECT ANSWER IN THE SPACE AT THE RIGHT.*

1. A war veteran in need of public assistance and care who applies for such relief in this city will be eligible to receive such help if he 1.____
   A. had been discharged from military service only under honorable conditions
   B. is a resident of this city on the date of application for public assistance
   C. has been a state resident for a period of one year or more
   D. was a resident of the city at the time he entered the military service

2. Mrs. Doe was receiving aid to dependent children for the third year when, in the course of reinvestigation, the social service worker discovered that she had a part-time job and arranged to reduce her relief accordingly. Mrs. Doe objected to the reduction and, after discussing her case with the proper officials in the Department of Social Services, decided to file a final appeal from their decision. 2.____
   A social service worker aware of the proper procedure to be followed in this case would have advised Mrs. Doe that the highest authority to which she could appeal is the
   A. Social Security Administration
   B. State Charities Aid
   C. Commissioner of Social Services
   D. State Department of Social Welfare

3. A social service worker receives complaints from neighbors that the three children of a certain relief family are being neglected by their parents to the point where their health and safety are endangered, and suggestions are made that the youngsters be separated from their negligent parents. 3.____
   Authority to order removal of the children from their home, if investigation substantiates these charges, is vested PRIMARILY in
   A. the Commissioner of Social Services
   B. the Society for the Prevention of Cruelty to Children
   C. a Family Court Judge
   D. a police officer

4. Anthony, aged 8, has had many difficult experiences in his life. His father's whereabouts are unknown as he deserted when Anthony was two years old. His mother, whom he loved dearly, died three months ago. Since that time he has been living with his grandmother, who is old and ill, and cannot care for such an active little boy. Together the grandmother and you, the social service worker, have decided that placement in a foster home is essential for Anthony's well-being. You know he will resist any change in his living arrangements. 4.____

According to acceptable case work practice, the BEST of the following methods for you to apply in this situation is to
- A. take the boy to his new home without telling him anything beforehand
- B. explain that it is necessary to move him and that he is going to a very nice place where he will be happy and have many things he does not have now
- C. tell him you are sorry if he feel bad about it, but grown-ups know best what is good for him and he will have to do what they say
- D. give the child a chance to get to know you before he is moved and to express his feelings in relation to the plan which is being made for him

5. Mrs. Mary Wooster, who has been caring for her 10-year-old orphaned niece, applies for aid to dependent children when her husband's income is reduced. If you are the social worker assigned to this case, you should tell Mrs. Wooster that her application 5.____
   - A. *cannot be accepted* for investigation because her niece must be removed from her home and placed out by the state
   - B. *can be accepted* for investigation because she falls within the group of relatives who are eligible to receive aid to dependent children
   - C. *cannot be accepted* for investigation because relatives other than parents are never granted help through aid to dependent children
   - D. *can be accepted* for investigation because her niece is her legal responsibility

6. A 15-year-old girl calls on you, the social service worker, to say that her mother is negligent and buys clothing for herself and treats her male friends to motion picture dates with her grant from aid to dependent children. 6.____
   According to the MOST generally accepted social case work principles, you should tell the girl that
   - A. the grant will be stopped immediately
   - B. she does not have to put up with that kind of environment and can arrange to leave her mother immediately
   - C. you will take this matter up with her mother and see her again at some future time
   - D. she should file a formal complaint against her mother

7. Assume that in making your first visit to the home of an applicant for aid to dependent children, you find the beds unmade, the dishes unwashed, and the furniture so dusty that you cannot find a clean place to sit down, although it is already 3:00 in the afternoon. The applicant has four small children. 7.____
   Under the circumstances described, you should inform the applicant that
   - A. she is ineligible for the grant because she does not give her children the proper physical environment
   - B. her application will be investigated and her eligibility determined
   - C. her application will be investigated but if her home is not cleaned up when you visit next week, her application will be rejected
   - D. if found eligible for aid to dependent children, she must take instruction in housekeeping from the social services center home economist

8. One of your clients finds it necessary to be away from home for two weeks and arranges with her mother to care for her children, for whom she receives an aid to dependent children grant, without notifying your department about this plan. You discover her absence, however, when making a periodic revisit to the client's apartment.
   In view of these facts, it would be MOST advisable to
   A. stop the grant immediately inasmuch as you are unable to see the client at this time
   B. let the grant continue, as the temporary planned absence of the client does affect her eligibility
   C. tell the client's mother that a recipient of aid to dependent children may not leave her children even for a temporary period
   D. order the client's mother to wire her to return within two days or the grant will stop

9. When a relief recipient requests that the Department of Social Services take some action because her unemployed husband is indifferent to her and unconcerned about the welfare of their children, the social service worker should
   A. inform the husband that he will be cut out of the grant if he does not change his attitude
   B. advise the woman to separate and try to build a life apart from her husband
   C. tell the woman to appeal to the Domestic Relations Court to have her husband ordered to spend his evenings at home
   D. suggest that the woman discuss this matter with a private family agency

10. A woman appears at your social services center and asks for advice on what to do as she would like, if possible, to be able to remain at home with her three children, aged four, seven, and ten. She declares that her husband has been killed and she is unable to manage on her old age and survivors insurance. Assuming the facts to be true as stated, the social service worker should advise her
    A. to apply for aid to dependent children
    B. to try to find a job
    C. to apply for more money under old age and survivors insurance
    D. that there are no other public financial resources available in her case

11. A child born out of wedlock to a certain Miss Smith has been placed in a private foster home. Miss Smith is unable to pay anything toward the child's care and one day, in discussing the case with a worker at the Bureau of Child Welfare, she asks about visiting her little girl.
    The MOST desirable reply for the social service worker to make in his situation would be that Miss Smith
    A. cannot visit the child because she would exert an adverse influence over her
    B. should not visit since she is not paying for the child's care

C. should not visit because it will be difficult for the child to explain to her friends that her mother is unmarried
D. has the same right as any other mother to visit her child

12. Eight-year-old Johnny, on whose account his mother is receiving aid to dependent children, is beginning to truant from school. Disturbed by the course of events, his mother appears at the social services center and informs you, her social service worker, that her efforts to stop Johnny's truancy have been unavailing.
You should tell Johnny's mother that
    A. the grant will be discontinued since Johnny's truancy is evidence of her failure as a parent
    B. she can be referred to a specialized agency in the community
    C. you will institute court action to remove Johnny from his home environment
    D. you will give her two months to straighten out the problem before taking further action

13. Suppose you, as social service worker, are considering institutional care for several different types of children for whom removal from present homes is indicated.
Of the following, the type LEAST suited for such care would be
    A. a child needing observation, study, and treatment for a severe crippling condition
    B. a 15-year-old boy who resents adult authority
    C. a family of six brothers and sisters who are devoted to each other
    D. a normal 3-year-old girl whose mother is dead and whose father is employed at night

14. It is generally agreed among psychologists that children need to have certain experiences in order to develop into healthy, well-integrated adults.
Of the following, it is MOST important to the development of the pre-adolescent child that he
    A. live in a good neighborhood
    B. have a room of his own
    C. have nice clothes
    D. have the feeling that he is loved and wanted by his parents

15. The only educative agency which can properly be thought of as really starting with a *clean slate* in developing a person's behavior is the
    A. family   B. play group
    C. church group   D. elementary school

16. The LEAST accurate of the following statements regarding intelligence is that
    A. a person's intelligence is not directly related to biological factors
    B. persons differ radically in the degree of intelligence which they have
    C. persons cannot learn beyond the limits of their native intelligence regardless of the amount and kind of effort they expend

D. ill health, isolation, and certain kinds of temperament may seriously limit the proportion of one's intelligence which he may actually be able to put to use

17. The GREATEST limitation on the general effectiveness of marriage courses in college curricula is
    A. there is no evidence to prove that such courses result in better matings and happier homes
    B. successful completion of such courses is no indication that the knowledge contained in the courses will be successfully applied by the students who have taken them
    C. there is no complete agreement as to whether the family, the church, or the school should be responsible for guiding marriage education
    D. most of the people who marry are ineligible to enroll in such courses

17.____

18. In the following instances, cooperative behavior which results from loyalty to the same objective is BEST exemplified by
    A. the citizens of a community forming a committee for the purpose of building a school
    B. employer and employee agreeing to a conference for the purpose of arriving at an equitable wage settlement
    C. people attending a championship tennis match held for charitable purposes
    D. during WWII, the citizens of a German community accepting employment in the local headquarters of the American Military Government

18.____

19. Among persons handicapped by blindness, the ones who may be expected to display a range of experience MOST comparable with that of normal persons are those who
    A. receive no special consideration from others
    B. are closely protected by their kinsmen and friends against the severe limitations imposed by their handicap
    C. are urged to greater attainments than would be expected of normal persons in order to compensate for their affliction
    D. are urged to understand their potentialities and limitations and are encouraged to make the most of their opportunities

19.____

20. From the social service point of view, the MOST desirable requisite for a potential social service worker to have at the outset is
    A. a desire to return full value for the taxpayer's dollar
    B. knowledge of eligibility requirements for relief
    C. understanding of the functions of the Department of Social Services
    D. a desire to help people meet their problems

20.____

21. From the case history on a client described as a delinquent individual, illiterate, shy, regarded by others with annoyance or condescension, who hardly ever engages in group activities and never goes to church, movies, or theater, the social service worker would be justified in forming the conclusion that

21.____

A. the social isolation is responsible for the delinquency
B. the delinquency is responsible for the social isolation
C. both the poverty and isolation are responsible for the delinquency
D. a single case is insufficient for the inference that social isolation is regularly associated with poverty and delinquency

22. If a repatriated citizen disembarks at the Port of New York in a destitute condition, his relief problem will be handled in the following manner: he will be cared for by the
    A. Department of Social Services and the Federal Security Agency will reimburse the city in full for the expense involved
    B. Department of Social Services and the State Board of Social Welfare will reimburse the city in full for the expense involved
    C. Department of Social Services and the State will reimburse the city for 80% of the expense involved
    D. Immigration and Naturalization Service without cost to the city

22.____

23. In the past, census figures sometimes showed that in the age groups from 55 up, the number of foreign-born in the United States was greater than would ordinarily be expected in our population.
    The MOST reliable explanation for this condition was probably that
    A. foreigners outlived native Americans because only the hardier among them ventured to emigrate from their own countries
    B. there were comparatively few young people among the foreign-born because immigration had been materially reduced
    C. foreign-born children had a shorter life expectancy than native-born children of foreign or American parents
    D. the number of persons who emigrated from the United States to other countries at those times exceeded the number who entered this country in the same period

23.____

24. A small town without a hospital is located near a large city which boasts of its excellent medical facilities. These facilities are extended liberally to non-residents who come from adjacent centers which do not have hospitals of their own.
    If it is shown statistically that the death rate of the small town is lower compared to that of the large city, the MOST logical inference for the alert social service worker to make is that
    A. small-town life is more healthful than living in a big city
    B. the statistical data have been improperly manipulated
    C. death rates should not be determined by political boundaries
    D. the deaths of non-residents have boosted the death rate of the large city

24.____

25. Of the types of mental breakdown listed below, the disorder that ordinarily occurs at the MOST advanced age is
    A. cerebral arteriosclerosis   B. neurasthenia
    C. dementia praecox   D. paresis

25.____

26. The parole movement for releasing prisoners before the expiration of their sentence has gained headway MOSTLY because of the assumption on the part of the taxpaying public that
    A. prison officials and parole officers can watch the paroled prisoner closely and help him adjust himself in the community at the same time
    B. recidivism is greater for persons serving their full sentence
    C. it sends the parolee out with an obligation rather than a score to settle
    D. total costs for prison administration are materially reduced when a large percentage of the prison population have their terms of incarceration reduced

27. Among the theories advanced in favor of providing unemployment relief, the one that should appear to the social service worker as MOST basic is that
    A. it is the responsible of the government to provide for those unable to provide for themselves
    B. people would work for very little and thereby bring down salaries if unemployment relief were not granted
    C. a wholesome economy can exist only when money is kept circulating
    D. every man has the right to a job

28. During a period of economic adjustment when unemployment is on the rise, the invention of a labor-saving device would, in the long run, be economically and culturally
    A. *unsound*, because it would stir up unrest among the organized labor groups
    B. *unsound*, because it would result in accelerating unemployment
    C. *sound*, because the rise of unemployment is a temporary phenomenon while the labor-saving device would add permanent values
    D. *sound*, because it would enable the user to produce more with the small working population still employed

29. Wage rates for women in the United States do not match those for men in many industries LARGELY because
    A. women tend to constitute a marginal supply of labor
    B. the social attitude has swung back to the position that *women's place is in the home*
    C. the organized labor movement has modified its traditional stand regarding *equal pay for equal work*
    D. women do not attain highly responsible positions in the business world as consistently as men

30. The inability of people to obtain employment during a time of economic depression is an example of the principle that
    A. anyone who really wants a job can get one if he tries hard enough
    B. the more capable people get jobs when jobs are scarce
    C. at certain times, employment is not available for many people irrespective of ability, character, or need
    D. full employment is a thing of the past

KEY (CORRECT ANSWERS)

1.	B	11.	D	21.	D
2.	D	12.	B	22.	A
3.	C	13.	D	23.	B
4.	D	14.	D	24.	D
5.	B	15.	A	25.	A
6.	C	16.	A	26.	A
7.	B	17.	D	27.	A
8.	B	18.	A	28.	C
9.	D	19.	D	29.	D
10.	A	20.	D	30.	C

TEST 3

DIRECTIONS: Each question or incomplete statement is followed by several suggested answers or completions. Select the one that BEST answers the question or completes the statement. *PRINT THE LETTER OF THE CORRECT ANSWER IN THE SPACE AT THE RIGHT.*

1. It is often held that cooperative activity is difficult to achieve because *individuals are basically selfish* and their alleged selfishness makes it difficult, if not impossible, to subordinate their individual wills to the collective enterprise.
   The CHIEF factor overlooked in such a conception of the matter is that
   A. there is no necessary discrepancy or conflict between selfishness and cooperation
   B. people do not seek to further their self-interest by competitive activity
   C. competition and cooperation are essentially alike
   D. most successful people are not selfish

   1.____

2. Under the law it is always necessary to establish eligibility for public assistance. While the facts that must be established are clearly defined by law and by policy, the social service worker has a good deal of freedom in his choice of method.
   Of the methods given below for obtaining desired information from applicants for relief, the one considered the BEST interviewing method in social work practice, and therefore recommended to the social service worker is to
   A. work from an outline, asking the questions in the order in which they appear and requiring the applicant to give specific answers
   B. let the applicant tell what he has to say in his own way first, the social service worker then taking responsibility for asking questions on points not covered
   C. tell the applicant all the facts that it is necessary to have, then letting him give the information in any way he chooses
   D. verify all such facts as birth date, income, and past employment before seeing the applicant, then asking the applicant to fill in the remaining gaps when he is interviewed.

   2.____

3. Suppose an applicant for relief objects to answering a question regarding his recent employment and asks, *What business is it of yours, young man?*
   As the social service worker conducting the interview, the MOST constructive course of action for you to take under the circumstances would be to
   A. tell the applicant you have no intention of prying into his personal affairs and go on to the next question
   B. refer the applicant to your supervisor
   C. rephrase the question so that only a *Yes* or *No* answer is required
   D. explain why the question is being asked

   3.____

2 (#3)

4. Continued contact with relief recipients is maintained by social service workers employed by the Department of Social Services MAINLY because
   A. changes in relief need to be made in accordance with financial changes in the family situation
   B. many people do not report changes in income promptly
   C. most people do not understand that reports of their earnings are required
   D. the department wishes to see that the relief given is properly used

4.____

5. Inasmuch as periodic visits to clients at home are required by the Department of Social Services, according to good case work practice, it is MOST desirable for the social service worker to
   A. visit without appointment as this gives him a chance to see the person and the house *as they really are* and forestalls changing things to create a different impression
   B. write giving an appointment time as this saves the social worker from visiting when people are not home and helps him to plan his work more efficiently
   C. write suggesting an appointment time so that the client may be prepared for the interview and the social worker uses his time economically
   D. advise all applicant during their first interview that they will be visited periodically but not be given definite appointments

5.____

6. Assuming that careful interpretation has been given but an applicant for public assistance refuses to accede to the necessary procedures to establish his eligibility for aid, the MOST preferable of the following courses of action for you to take would be to
   A. do nothing further
   B. grant temporary aid in the hope that the applicant will change his mind
   C. try to ascertain why the applicant feels as he does, but to respect his decision if he refuses to change his mind
   D. proceed to check on all the facts possible even though the applicant has not given his permission

6.____

7. The PRIMARY purpose in discussing with an applicant steps in determining his eligibility and the kind of verification of facts which the agency will need is to
   A. enable the applicant to understand the basis of eligibility and participate in determining it
   B. protect the position of the agency so that there will be no comeback if relief is not granted
   C. give the applicant an opportunity to modify any statement he may have made previously
   D. promote public relations for the agency, since the applicant will tell others how the agency is operating

7.____

8. The BEST of the following reasons for which a public social services agency should NOT insist on certain standards of cleanliness as a factor in eligibility to receive relief is that it is generally acknowledged that
   A. people have a right to decide how they will live, provided their mode of living does not hurt others

8.____

B. standards of cleanliness vary so much among people as to make one standard impracticable
C. a little dirt has never hurt anyone
D. it would take too much of the social service worker's time to maintain a constant check on this factor

9. When a client receives home relief, he
   A. gives up the right to manage his money in his own way
   B. is justified in assuming that he has proved his eligibility for relief and is free to use the money according to his best judgment
   C. is limited in spending the money only for expenditures itemized in the agency budget
   D. is obligated to keep an itemized list of his expenditures

10. The knowledge and understanding of situations and of people attained through social case work may well serve as a basis for sound action and for effective social welfare planning.
    The MOST logical assumption that the social service worker can draw from the above statement is that
    A. since social service planning is related to broad social issues and needs, it is unnecessary to consider the individual
    B. the individual is the only unit to be considered in the planning of effective social welfare programs
    C. all social planning should be directed primarily toward the individual and his needs
    D. knowledge of the individual attained through social case work can be effectively utilized in planning a broad social welfare program

11. Of the following, the LEAST valid reason for the maintenance of the case record in public social services administration is to
    A. furnish reference material for other workers
    B. improve the quality of service to the client
    C. show how the public funds are being expended
    D. reduce the complexities of the case to manageable proportions

12. A public social services agency will lean more on forms than a private agency in the same field of activity because
    A. forms simplify the recording responsibilities of newly appointed social service workers
    B. public social service records are of the family agency type
    C. the governmental framework requires a greater degree of standardization
    D. more interviews and visits are made in connection with public relief cases

13. In spite of the need which most of us have of finding rules and procedures to guide us, we must face the difficulty at the outset that there is no such thing as a model case.
    Of the following, the BEST justification for this statement is that
    A. records should be written to suit the case
    B. case recording should be patterned after the best models obtainable

C. rules cannot be applied to social case work because each case requires individual treatment
D. the establishment of routine and procedures in social work is an ideal which cannot be realized

14. One of the following disclosures is made regarding an applicant for old-age assistance and he is accordingly disqualified to receive the grant requested. In the recommendation submitted by the social service worker, the applicant would be found ineligible because he
    A. is not a citizen
    B. has $1,000 in a bank account which he is saving for burial purposes
    C. has three married children and could probably live with one of them
    D. refuses to give information concerning a bank account of $50,000 which had been in his name until four months prior to his application

15. The homemaking center of the Department of Social Services furnishes the service of mother's aides to families for help in caring for their children because of the mother's temporary incapacity or absence. Mother's aides can assume responsibility for such household duties as feeding infants, preparing meals, cleaning the home, etc. They are mature, responsible women with previous homemaking experience who have passed a literacy test and have undergone a thorough physical examination.
    According to current thinking in the field, for the social service worker assigned in any case where a mother's aide is furnished, to use the mother's aide as a source of obtaining confidential information for the Department of Social Services would be
    A. *advisable*; as a result of contact with the family, the mother's aide will have observed many details concerning their daily activities
    B. *inadvisable*; while the mother's aide will have observed many details concerning the daily activities of the family, she has not been trained to interpret these observations
    C. *advisable*; the mother's aide has been thoroughly examined as to her ability to perform her duties in the household
    D. *inadvisable*; the mother's aide has a primary obligation to the family rather than to the Department of Social Services

16. When a family asks the help of the social service worker because they are consistently exceeding their food and clothing allowance, the social service worker should
    A. use the services of the home economist for consultation on the management problem which has developed
    B. order the family to live within their budget allowance
    C. ignore the situation as it is the family's responsibility to make ends meet
    D. recommend small increases in the food and clothing allowance for this family

17. When a landlord complains to the social service worker that a certain relief recipient has consistently neglected to pay his rent, present case work practice would indicate to the social service worker that he should FIRST
    A. arrange to discontinue relief payments until he can verify the reasons for the non-payment of rent
    B. tell the client to pay his rent within a certain period of time if he does not want his relief discontinued
    C. tell the client about the landlord's complaint and inform him the Department of Social Services assumes that rent is an obligation the client is expected to settle directly with his landlord
    D. arrange for the landlord to collect his rent at the social services center in the future

Questions 18-23.

DIRECTIONS: Questions 18 through 23, inclusive, deal with social service allowances of various kinds. Assuming that in the Department of Social Services the allowance schedules shown below are among those included in estimating the needs of relief recipients, use the figures given to determine your answers. All figure are quoted on a monthly basis.

Item	Allowance
Rent	As paid by client
Utilities	$12 per person
Person Incidentals	$7 per person

	Adult	Child 13-18	Child Under 13
Food	$360	$350	$300
Clothing	90	84	79

18. The Anderson family consisting of father, mother, and four children aged 4, 10, 15, and 17, is eligible for home relief. The rent is $800 a month. Relief granted on the basis of the above items is given semi-monthly.
    According to the above schedule, the proper semi-monthly grant for this family would be
    A. $1,076   B. $1,427   C. $1,717   D. $3,134

19. Assuming that all the expenditures except rent were reimbursed under the State Welfare Law to the same extent that reimbursements for home relief are now being made to the city, the annual cost to the city for all the items included in the public assistance budget of the Anderson family would be APPROXIMATELY
    A. $8,400   B. $16,000   C. $24,000   D. $28,000

6 (#3)

20. Mrs. Peet is 67 years old and applies for old-age assistance. She lives with her widowed niece who has a family of three children. The rent of the apartment is $560 a month. The niece has agreed to pay for the utilities of the whole group and also to give Mrs. Peet some money for personal incidentals, provided that Mrs. Peet can pay one-fifth of the rent. On medical advice, a special diet allowance of $77.20 a month is authorized for Mrs. Peet in addition to the regular food allowance.
The proper monthly grant for Mrs. Peet would be
   A. $498.80   B. $560.75   C. $639.20   D. $1,006.50

20.____

21. Mrs. Scalise applies for relief for herself and her two children aged two and four. Her rent costs $650 a month. She is separated from her husband, who contributes $180 a week by court order. It has also been verified that Mrs. Scalise earns $112 a week doing piece-work at home.
Assuming that for budget computation purposes the Department of Social Services considers 4.3 weeks as equivalent to one month, the monthly grant in this case would be
   A. $538.10   B. $659.40   C. $938.00   D. $1,012.20

21.____

22. A 36-year-old sightless widower applies for aid to the blind. His rent and utilities are met by relatives with whom he lives. In aid to blind cases, $92 per month is allowed for expenses incident to blindness as a substitute for the personal incidentals item in the above schedule.
Under these circumstances, the proper monthly grant would be
   A. $342.50   B. $537.00   C. $646.50   D. $1,057.50

22.____

23. John Burke is 52 years old and needs supplementary home relief. He pays $370 a month for his room and he earn $420 a month doing odd jobs.
Basing your computations on these facts and on the above schedule, you can determine that the proper semi-monthly grant for Mr. Burke would be
   A. $508.50   B. $369.60   C. $209.50   D. $163.00

23.____

24. In attempting to discover whether an applicant for aid to dependent children has had any previous experience as a relief recipient through other social service agencies in the community, the social service worker should
   A. check the application for such aid with the social service exchange
   B. send the fingerprints of the applicant to the Police Department
   C. consult the latest records of the Department of Social Services
   D. ask the applicant to submit a notarized statement to the effect that such aid has not been received from any other source

24.____

25. Mr. Ritter asks the Department of Social Services to place his son, aged five, in a foster home. In a subsequent interview, Mr. Ritter refuses to divulge what sources of income are at his disposal.
As the social service worker trying to obtain this information, you should explain to Mr. Ritter that
   A. you want to know whether he is seeking placement for his son because he does not want to provide for him financially

25.____

B. part of placement procedure involves determining the extent of financial responsibility parents can continue to assume
C. if he makes no payment his parental rights will be affected
D. the frequency of his visits will depend on the amount of support he continues to furnish

26. A woman applying for supplementation of her earnings explains that she earns $300 weekly but that the doctor has advised her to work only four days a week in order to safeguard her health. Under the reduced schedule, her earnings would drop to $200 a week and she would be unable to continue supporting her 62-year-old mother.
Assuming that this information has been duly verified, the woman's request for supplementary relief should be
    A. *granted*, because she supports her old mother
    B. *not granted*, because she can still manage to work a full week
    C. *granted*, because the reduction of work is necessary to preserve her health
    D. *not granted*, because her mother can get old-age assistance

27. Suppose a client whom you are investigating has borrowed $250 in order to purchase an evening gown for one of her children who is being graduated from high school. She is planning to repay the loan at the rate of $10 a week, and presents verification of this transaction as well as of the purchase.
As a social service worker, you would be complying with the BEST case work principles by
    A. telling the client her grant will be reduced in view of her ability to manage on $10 less each week
    B. telling the clerk that she must never do this again
    C. explaining to the client how her action will make it more difficult for the family to get along on their limited grant
    D. suggesting that she return the dress and repay the borrowed money in this way

28. Mrs. Rose complains to the social service worker about the inadequacy of her relief allowance although she is being granted the maximum amount for a person in her situation. It is acknowledged by the Department of Social Services that the amount of the grant is not based on current prices.
Under these circumstances, the MOST considerate reply the social service worker can make to this complainant is that
    A. the grant is based on a scientific calculation of needs for subsistence and is only a small percentage short of what is actually needed
    B. the social service worker knows it is difficult to manage since the cost of living was steadily rising, but that the amount granted was all the Department of Social Services schedule allows at the present time
    C. Mrs. Rose would be worse off if there were no public assistance
    D. many people in other countries do not have even the small grant allowed Mrs. Rose

29. Miss Lowe applies for assistance and is able to account for her work history and her financial expenditures with the exception of three months in 2020.
As acting intake interviewer, it would be your responsibility to inform her that
    A. she will remain ineligible until she accounts for her complete work history
    B. her application can be accepted, but that certain verification will have to be made as to her statements regarding lack of resources
    C. she is obviously hiding pertinent information and that her application cannot therefore be considered
    D. she obviously had some sources in 2020 and that she should use this source again

30. Knowing that a client needs a period of rest and that another agency can arrange this, it would be the responsibility of a social service worker to
    A. notify the client of this resource and suggest that he apply there if he wishes to
    B. try to make all the arrangements for the client, telling the other agency he knows all about the client's situation and can apply for him
    C. tell the client that unless he applies to the other agency, he will do so for him
    D. tell the client he seems insufficiently interested in getting well enough to work and the Department of Social Services may discontinue his assistance

31. An irate citizen comes into the Social Services office protesting that William Case, a relief recipient, made no effort to shop most economically and was therefore wasting public funds which he, a taxpayer, in part contributed. The complainant wants to know why Mr. Case was given cash instead of a food voucher.
The social service worker should tell this citizen that the Department of Social Services will not transfer Mr. Case to voucher relief because cash relief
    A. is easier to administer
    B. enables the investigator to know how responsible a person is by the way he spends his money
    C. enables people to maintain their usual way of living
    D. keeps money in circulation

32. Assume that a certain Mr. Sears applied for relief three weeks ago. As he has not yet received an assistance, he comes to see the social service worker to find out why he is being neglected. A checkup of Mr. Sears' status reveals that his application has been inactive pending receipt of a reply from a former employer. When informed of this contingency, Mr. Sears offers to expedite matters by getting in touch with the employer himself.
The BEST way for the social service worker to handle this case would be to tell Mr. Sears that
    A. the determination of his eligibility is the responsibility of the social service worker alone
    B. it would help if he could hurry the reply
    C. if he discusses this with the employer, the information will be invalidated
    D. he should just go home and wait

33. When he applies for public relief, a man gives a complete and straightforward account of his past employment and earnings, of the inability of his relatives to help, and of his attempts to find work. The way the family has managed in the past indicates excellent planning ability in the use of money and making limited resources go a long way. He says he exhausted all resources before applying, and gives a detailed account. The family lived on less than a relief allowance while receiving unemployment compensation. They have exhausted their credit at the grocery store. The landlord is threatening eviction because of rent arrears of two months. He explains he went through all this because it is so painful for him to apply for relief. The man is obviously honest and reliable. Under these circumstances, a conscientious social service worker would find that
   A. it is unnecessary to verify the foregoing information in order to establish eligibility
   B. it is necessary to verify the facts given above in order to establish eligibility
   C. the interviewer should be free to decide whether any verifications are needed
   D. eligibility considerations should be waived and an immediate grant made in order to help the man feel better

34. Mr. Russell complains to his social service worker that he is too feeble to cook his own food and needs more money in order to eat in restaurants.
   If investigation of the request proves that Mr. Russell's condition is as indicated, the social service worker should
   A. explain why no provision can be made for this additional expense
   B. suggest that Mr. Russell get a neighbor to help with the cooking
   C. recommend that the allowance be increased
   D. explain that relief recipients should not eat in restaurants

35. When applying for unemployment relief, a prospective client states that he can get a job immediately at $300 a week but that he has hesitated to accept such employment because he feels his income would be inadequate to support his family which, besides himself, includes his wife and two children. The applicant also states that he has enrolled in a training program which, if he can pursue to a satisfactory conclusion two weeks hence, will enable him to accept a job paying $500 weekly.
   If you were the social service worker in this case, the MOST constructive of the following courses of action for you to take would be to
   A. recommend that relief be given immediately
   B. recommend that relief not be given because the applicant has a $300 job available to him
   C. tell the applicant he must take the $300 job and then give him supplementation on account of his inadequate earnings
   D. recommend relief if the information is verified

KEY (CORRECT ANSWERS)

1.	A	11.	D	21.	B	31.	C
2.	B	12.	C	22.	B	32.	B
3.	D	13.	A	23.	C	33.	B
4.	A	14.	D	24.	A	34.	C
5.	C	15.	B	25.	B	35.	D
6.	C	16.	A	26.	C		
7.	A	17.	C	27.	C		
8.	A	18.	C	28.	B		
9.	B	19.	B	29.	B		
10.	D	20.	C	30.	A		

EXAMINATION SECTION
TEST 1

DIRECTIONS: Each question or incomplete statement is followed by several suggested answers or completions. Select the one that BEST answers the question or completes the statement. *PRINT THE LETTER OF THE CORRECT ANSWER IN THE SPACE AT THE RIGHT.*

1. In handling a case, an investigator should summarize the facts he has gathered and the observations he has made about the family and incorporate this material into a formal social study of the family.
   Of the following, the CHIEF advantage of such a practice is that it will provide a(n)

   A. picture of the family on the basis of which evaluations and plans can be made
   B. easily accessible listing of the factors pertaining to eligibility
   C. simple and uniform method of recording the family's social history
   D. opportunity for the investigator to record his evaluation of the family's situation

2. An applicant for assistance tells the investigator that he has always supported himself by doing odd jobs.
   While attempting to verify the applicant's history of past maintenance, it is MOST important for the investigator to determine, in addition,

   A. how the applicant was able to obtain a sufficient number of odd jobs to support himself
   B. what skills the applicant had that enabled him to obtain these jobs
   C. why the applicant never sought or kept a steady job
   D. whether such jobs are still available as a source of income for the applicant

3. For an investigator to make a collateral contact with a client's legally responsible relative when that relative is herself receiving assistance is

   A. *advisable,* mainly because the relative may be able to assist the client with needed services
   B. *inadvisable,* mainly because the relative is in receipt of assistance and cannot assist the client financially
   C. *advisable,* mainly because the worker may obtain information concerning the relative's eligibility for assistance
   D. *inadvisable,* because any information concerning the relative can be obtained from other sources

4. An applicant for assistance tells the investigator that her bank savings are exhausted. While a bank clearance can verify her statement, it is still important for the investigator to see her bank book CHIEFLY in order to

   A. determine when the account was first opened and the amount of the initial deposit
   B. correlate withdrawals and deposits with the applicant's story of past management
   C. learn if the applicant had closed this account in order to open an account in another bank
   D. verify that the last withdrawal was made before the applicant applied for assistance

5. It has been suggested that all investigators be kept currently informed about general departmental actions taken, changes in other departmental work units, and new developments of general interest in their department.
For a department to put this suggestion into effect is, generally,

   A. *inadvisable;* investigators should perform the duties specifically assigned to them and not get involved in matters that do not concern them directly
   B. *advisable;* investigators may often need to know such information in order to coordinate their work properly with that of other work units
   C. *inadvisable;* changes in other work units have little effect on the work performed by investigators not assigned to these units
   D. *advisable;* broad knowledge of the activities in any agency tends to improve work skills

6. Although there is a normal distinction between the successive ranks of supervision in an agency, the greatest distinction and change in rank occurs, however, when an investigator becomes a supervisor.
This is true CHIEFLY because the supervisor

   A. must be better informed than his investigators in all aspects
   B. must learn to assume new and more complex duties
   C. becomes responsible for the first time for the job performance of members of the investigation staff
   D. has greater responsibility and authority than the investigators under his supervision

7. When an experienced supervisory investigator does not agree personally with some of the procedurally correct objectives and directions of his supervisor, it would be MOST correct for him to

   A. continue to supervise his unit in accordance with the supervisor's directions
   B. direct his workers to follow the supervisor's directions, but indicate the weaknesses therein and be somewhat more lenient in the supervision of these duties
   C. seek to change the supervisor's directions through use of grievance procedures
   D. develop his own methods and apply them to the work of his unit on a trial basis

8. It has been said that the success or failure of the work of his unit rests on the supervisor.
If the supervisor wants to stimulate growth among his investigators, it would generally be BEST for him to

   A. set an easy pace for his investigators so that they will not become confused because of having to learn too much too rapidly
   B. set the pace for his investigators so that the job is never too easy but is a constant challenge calling for more and better work
   C. spot check the investigators' records at irregular intervals in order to determine whether they are performing their duties properly
   D. see to it that the broad objectives and goals of the department are periodically communicated and interpreted to his investigators

9. The effectiveness of the work of a unit of investigators depends in a large measure on that unit's will to work.
The BEST of the following methods for the supervisor to employ in order to increase the will of the members of the unit to work is for the unit supervisor to

A. allow each investigator to proceed at his own pace
B. be constantly on guard for any laxity among his investigators
C. provide comfortable working facilities for his investigators
D. clearly discuss with his investigators the functions and objectives of the agency

10. For a supervisor to encourage his investigators to think about the reasons for a policy is

    A. *advisable,* mainly because the investigators are then more likely to apply the policy appropriately
    B. *inadvisable,* mainly because the investigators may then apply the policy too flexibly
    C. *advisable,* mainly because the investigators then feel that they have participated in policy making
    D. *inadvisable,* mainly because the investigators may interpret the policy incorrectly if they misunderstand its meaning

11. A supervisor who plans his work properly and who has no difficulty in meeting deadlines insists that his new investigators pattern their activities after his in every detail.
    This method is

    A. *undesirable,* chiefly because such compliance can cause antagonism and hamper the investigators' growth
    B. *undesirable,* chiefly because this method cannot work as successfully for the new investigators
    C. *desirable,* chiefly because the supervisor's methods have proved successful and will eliminate waste
    D. *desirable,* chiefly because the untrained investigator needs guidelines to follow

12. Of the following, the MOST important reason for obtaining information in an initial investigation regarding financial maintenance of the applicant prior to the application for assistance is to

    A. comply with the provisions in the Social Welfare Law requiring that a record be made of the financial history of applicants for public assistance
    B. determine if the applicant may be expected to handle properly public assistance grants in the form of money
    C. determine the way in which the present situation differs from the past
    D. show the applicant that the department is interested in his past and present circumstances and may be expected to maintain this interest in the future

13. An applicant for assistance who has legally responsible relatives is informed by the investigator of the responsibility of such relatives to contribute to the applicant's support. The applicant requests permission to discuss the matter privately with these relatives prior to any contact by the department.
    In this case, it would be ADVISABLE for the investigator to

    A. *agree* to the request because the applicant is entitled to an opportunity to prepare the relatives for the coming official contact
    B. *agree* to the request because the applicant is in a better position than the investigator to uncover any concealment of assets by his relatives
    C. *refuse* the request because it might give the applicant and his relatives opportunity to devise means of avoiding or minimizing the existing responsibility
    D. *refuse* the request because the applicant is not likely to be able to give a proper interpretation to the relatives of their responsibility

14. The findings of a medical examination of a client who has claimed to be unemployable because of physical illness are that the client is employable. When told of these findings, the client reiterates that she is too ill to work.
In this case, the BEST of the following actions for the investigator to take FIRST is to

    A. discuss the situation with the client in an attempt to discover what reasons she may have for not wanting to accept employment
    B. make arrangements for a psychiatric examination of the client
    C. request that a second medical examination of the client be made by another doctor
    D. tell the client that the case will be closed unless she accepts employment

15. An investigator is told by a relative of a recipient that the recipient has won $6000 in a lottery and is soon to receive the prize money.
Of the following, the BEST action for the investigator to take FIRST is to

    A. close the case since the recipient did not notify the department of his winnings and since he now has enough money on which to live and pay his bills
    B. discuss the situation with the recipient, planning with him the future management of his funds
    C. let the recipient know that the use of relief money for gambling is illegal and that the police department must be notified of the facts in the case
    D. see that legal steps are taken to recover for services rendered to the client by the department.

16. When told at an interview with the investigator that he must agree to give to the department a lien on his real estate property, a client assumes a resistant attitude.
Of the following, it would usually be BEST for the investigator to

    A. discuss with the client the laws governing the giving of such liens and the purposes to be served by his giving the lien
    B. drop the matter, hoping to meet with less resistance at some future time
    C. tell the client that this is not a matter for discussion, that he must either agree to the lien or the case will be closed
    D. terminate the interview, telling the client that he may return when he is willing to discuss the means of providing the department with the lien

17. An investigator refers to his supervisor an applicant for assistance who has refused to supply certain information which is regularly asked of applicants. The applicant complains that he is being asked to supply private and personal information about himself that has nothing to do with his application for assistance and that the investigator has treated him with discourtesy.
The BEST of the following courses of action for the supervisor to take is to

    A. apologize for any appearance of discourtesy but insist that the applicant supply him with the information that had been sought
    B. apologize for any appearance of discourtesy, explain the need for the information that has been requested, and ask the applicant to supply it to the investigator
    C. explain that the investigator is doing a difficult job under difficult conditions and instruct the applicant to cooperate with him
    D. explain why the information is needed and state that no assistance will be forthcoming unless it is supplied

18. At an interview, in order to secure as efficiently as possible the information necessary to determine whether an applicant for assistance is eligible, investigators should generally be instructed to

    A. allow the applicant to explain his problem without interrupting him and then ask him to answer a previously prepared list of detailed questions covering necessary information
    B. confine the interview to a set of detailed questions prepared in advance by the investigator except that new questions may be added on the basis of leads provided by the answers to previous questions
    C. permit the applicant to explain his problems, using questions to keep the applicant from wandering from the subject and to bring out necessary information not covered by him in his narrative
    D. supply the applicant with a set of written questions immediately prior to the interview and confine the interview to a discussion of these questions

19. Assume that a client believes that his case has been unfairly closed, in spite of the fact that the investigator has explained the pertinent rules to him.
    It would be MOST proper, at this point, for the investigator to refer this client to

    A. an assistant to the commissioner at the central office
    B. an official of the state
    C. the supervisor in charge
    D. the supervisor in charge of the unit

20. An investigator is told by a client who is a resident of a nursing home that he is being neglected and not receiving proper care in the home.
    The investigator should

    A. discuss the situation with the proprietor of the nursing home
    B. investigate the situation on subsequent visits to determine the validity of the complaint
    C. report the matter to the medical social worker upon return to his center
    D. write a memorandum to the central nursing home service reporting the situation

21. Modern thinking and research on the efficient conduct of business has developed concepts of democratic supervision and human relations.
    Proper application of these concepts in dealing with investigators USUALLY results in

    A. a reduction in the use of formal discipline
    B. an increase in the use of formal discipline
    C. discarding discipline imposed from without to be completely replaced by self-imposed discipline
    D. elimination of formal discipline in favor of informal discipline

22. At the first interview between a supervisor and a newly appointed investigator, GREATEST care should be taken to

    A. build toward a satisfactory personal relationship even if some other objectives of the interview must be postponed
    B. cover a predetermined list of specific objectives so as to make a further orientation interview unnecessary

C. create an image of a forceful, determined supervisor whose wishes cannot be imposed by a subordinate without great risk
D. create an impression of efficiency and control of operation free from interpersonal relationships

23. In teaching the job to an investigator recently assigned to a unit, many teaching methods must be used.
In general, however, the BEST way for the supervisor to train such an investigator is by having him

   A. do the job under proper supervision
   B. listen to lectures
   C. observe the work of other investigators
   D. study written material

24. A recently appointed investigator has reached the stage in learning his job where he is just beginning to be able to make decisions, although he still makes numerous mistakes and frequently does not know how to handle a situation.
When the supervisor finds that the investigator has handled a certain situation in an acceptable manner, but not in the best manner, it would be BEST for the supervisor to

   A. explain to the investigator how he could have handled the situation better
   B. indicate approval of the way the situation was handled and explain how it could have been handled better
   C. say nothing about the situation
   D. show dissatisfaction with the way the situation was handled and explain how it could have been handled better

25. A supervisor has a job to be done of a type usually done by an investigator. The job is an important and recurring one, but not urgent at the moment. He knows that it would take more time to tell the investigator how to do the job than to do it himself, and that it would take still more time to make the investigator understand the situation, decide how to handle it, and then get the job done.
In such a case, it would generally be BEST for the supervisor to

   A. assign the job to the investigator without explaining it
   B. do the job himself
   C. explain the situation and help the investigator to decide how to handle it
   D. tell the investigator exactly what to do

KEY (CORRECT ANSWERS)

1. A
2. D
3. A
4. B
5. B

6. C
7. A
8. B
9. D
10. A

11. A
12. C
13. A
14. A
15. B

16. A
17. B
18. C
19. D
20. D

21. A
22. A
23. A
24. B
25. C

TEST 2

DIRECTIONS: Each question or incomplete statement is followed by several suggested answers or completions. Select the one that BEST answers the question or completes the statement. *PRINT THE LETTER OF THE CORRECT ANSWER IN THE SPACE AT THE RIGHT.*

1. In order to improve the work of an experienced investigator who usually does average work, the one of the following actions which it would generally be BEST for the supervisor to take is to

    A. allow the investigator to be self-directed and unsupervised except where there is a large outlay of money involved
    B. apply strict discipline to any signs of laxness or inattention to duty
    C. carefully list and document every error made by the investigator and inform him of them
    D. use praise as a device to motivate the investigator to do better work

2. The one of the following guiding principles to which a supervisor should give MOST consideration when it becomes necessary to discipline an investigator is that

    A. rules should be applied in a fixed and inflexible manner
    B. the discipline should be applied for the purpose of improving the morale of all his investigators
    C. the main benefit to be derived from disciplining one offender is to deter other potential offenders
    D. the nature of the discipline should be such as to improve the future work of the offender

3. A unit supervisor notices one of his investigators reading a novel at his desk during working hours. This is the first time that this has happened. The investigator is an experienced employee who does above-average work.
For the unit supervisor to ignore the situation is GENERALLY

    A. *wise*, since it is never desirable to penalize a good employee because of any single incident
    B. *unwise*, since it may be interpreted by the staff as condoning inattention to work
    C. *wise*, since democratic supervision allows employees leeway to apportion their workday as they see fit
    D. *unwise*, since it is necessary to take strong action at the first sign of insubordination

4. When investigators in a particular unit are guilty of infractions, it is the practice of the unit supervisor to give necessary warnings or reprimands in a jocular manner. This practice is GENERALLY

    A. *unwise*, because humorous or jocular aspects should be kept from relationships between supervisors and investigators
    B. *unwise*, because it leaves the investigator unsure of the true intent or extent of the discipline
    C. *wise*, because it makes the investigator realize that there is no personal animosity involved
    D. *wise*, because it reduces the severity of the warning or reprimand

50

5. An experienced investigator complains to his unit supervisor that the latter's continual very close supervision of his work is unnecessary and annoying. The unit supervisor is a recently appointed supervisor.
   In this case, it would generally be BEST for the unit supervisor to

   A. ask the investigator to explain his complaint further, telling him that it will receive consideration, and then re-evaluate his supervisory practices, seeking advice from his own supervisor if necessary
   B. assure the investigator that there had been no intention of singling him out but that, as a subordinate, he will have to get used to new supervisory methods employed by new, wide-awake supervisors
   C. explain to the investigator that it is the job of the unit supervisor to supervise him and that he should understand his role and be able to overcome his annoyance
   D. promise the investigator that the annoying supervisory methods will be discontinued but remind him that the unit supervisor must be respected and looked to for assistance, training, and supervision

6. A unit supervisor becomes aware that one of his investigators has a personal problem which is causing the subordinate considerable concern and is beginning to affect his work.
   Of the following, the action which it would generally be BEST for the unit supervisor to take is to

   A. ignore the matter but, if the investigator brings the matter up, politely tell him that it is not proper for a unit supervisor to discuss personal problems of subordinates
   B. make the investigator aware that he may discuss personal problems with his unit supervisor who will offer whatever assistance he can, compatible with the duties of his job
   C. refer the matter to his own supervisor
   D. indicate that he would like to help solve the problem and insist that the investigator provide full details

7. An investigator who has many personal problems frequently introduces one or more of them into the discussion at conferences with his unit supervisor. He talks of them at some length.
   It would generally be BEST for the unit supervisor to

   A. discuss the problems with the investigator and, as a helping person, assist with their solution
   B. explain that he would like to help solve the problems but that the repeated introduction of them in conferences is interfering with the work of the unit
   C. inform the investigator that his personal problems should not be brought to the office and that it would be improper for the unit supervisor to try to help with them
   D. listen silently to the exposition of the problems made by the investigator and then return to the business at hand without commenting on the problem

8. For the investigator to understand the culture of a family is important CHIEFLY because the

   A. client tends to react to the situation largely in ways derived from attitudes learned at home

B. needs of the entire family cannot be satisfied unless the individual needs of each member are satisfied first
C. client can be treated more effectively when considered as a member of a cultural group rather than a separate individual
D. family can be understood much more readily if the dominant individual motivating it is understood first

9. Emphasis in the practice of casework has shifted from merely providing the client with a practical service, to involving the client in using the service or treatment.
This statement implies MOST NEARLY that, at present,

    A. casework will attempt to help the client only when it is felt that he will profit from the service
    B. casework is no longer deeply involved in assisting the client in a direct and realistic way
    C. the most important change in casework today has been its shift from helping the client in a practical way to planning for him in a theoretical way
    D. the caseworker or investigator attempts to mobilize the client to active participation in decision-making

10. In all casework practice, whether it be in an agency or in an institution, the properly prepared case history record is of great importance in the treatment of the client and his problem CHIEFLY because it

    A. gives the supervisory and administrative casework staff reviewing the case a keener understanding of the general sociological and psychological causes underlying dependency and other factors which make it necessary for clients to seek casework assistance
    B. furnishes the agency or institution involved in the case with a factual record as a basis for determining whether or not continuing treatment of the client is justified
    C. assists the caseworkers or investigators involved in the case by providing them, on a continuous basis, with a clear picture of the various factors underlying the client's problems and of what has been done to help resolve the situation
    D. provides the caseworker or investigator responsible for the case with the basic facts which will enable her to determine whether the client is really trying to help himself or whether he is passing his responsibility on to the caseworker or investigator

11. When comparing the narrative form with the summary form of a casework recording, the narrative form is usually the BEST way to record

    A. objective material obtained from investigations of the client's statements, while the summary form is best to record worker's detailed observations of client's reactions to his present problem
    B. both social data and eligibility material, while the summary form is best to record material dealing with feelings, attitudes and client-worker relationships
    C. material relating to prognosis, treatment given, and the results obtained, while the summary form is best to record a verbatim report of primary evidence obtained from personal worker-client contacts
    D. material dealing with feelings, attitudes, and client-worker relationships, while the summary form is best to record both social data and eligibility material

12. A problem in recording is to decide how much detail to have in a case record. The case history should GENERALLY include

    A. a more detailed description of the client's reaction to practical matters than to psychological conflicts
    B. a verbatim account of worker-client interaction in significant interviews and a detailed description of the client's feelings toward the treatment plan
    C. only as much data, whether it be sociological or psychological, as will enable the worker to understand the client, the problem to be solved, and the main factors in its solution
    D. the full details of the client's personality development and emotional relationships regardless of the type or complexity of the problem

13. Interviewing is always directed to the client and his situation.
    The one of the following which is the MOST accurate statement with respect to the proper focus of an interview is that the

    A. investigator limits the client to concentration on objective data
    B. client is generally permitted to talk about facts and feelings with no direction from the investigator
    C. main focus in interviews is on feelings rather than facts
    D. investigator is responsible for helping the client focus on any material which seems to be related to his problems or difficulties

14. Assume that you are conducting a training program for the investigators under your supervision. At one of the sessions, you discuss the problem of interviewing a dull and stupid client who gives a slow and disconnected case history.
    The BEST of the following interviewing methods for you to recommend in such a case in order to ascertain the facts is for the investigator to

    A. ask the client leading questions requiring *yes* or *no* answers
    B. request the client to limit his narration to the essential facts so that the interview can be kept as brief as possible
    C. review the story with the client, patiently asking simple questions
    D. tell the client that unless he is more cooperative, he cannot be helped to solve his problem

15. A recent development in interviewing procedure, known as multiple-client interviewing, consists of interviews of the entire family at the same time. However, this may not be an effective method in certain situations.
    Of the following, the situation in which the standard individual interview would be PREFERABLE is when

    A. family members derive consistent and major gratification from assisting each other in their destructive responses
    B. there is a crucial family conflict to which the members are reacting
    C. the family is overwhelmed by interpersonal anxieties which have not been explored
    D. the investigator wants to determine the pattern of family interaction to further his diagnostic understanding

16. The one of the following which is the CHIEF value of verbatim recording of all or a portion of an important interview is the possibility it offers for

    A. careful study and clarification of psychological goals in treatment
    B. a prompt solution to the problem by preservation, in an orderly and concise fashion of the full psychological and economic picture of the client's situation
    C. quick determination of the more obvious social goals and offering of concrete services by presentation of the essential facts
    D. supervision of experienced investigators by showing the emotional overtones, subtle reactions, and intricate investigator-client interchanges

17. Experts in the field of casework recording generally agree that the kind of material for which the narrative form of recording is MOST suitable is

    A. material that deals with feelings, attitudes, and client-investigator relationships, because this style permits the use of primary evidence in the form of verbal material and behavior observed in the interview
    B. social data, including eligibility material and family background history, because it can then be presented in a chronological, orderly fashion to enable the investigator to select the desired facts
    C. personal facts concerning the individual's personality patterns and their growth and development, because they can be seen in an orderly progression from primal immaturity until their ultimate stage of completion
    D. selectively chosen and documented material essential to a quicker and clearer understanding of the various ramifications of the case by a new investigator when responsibility for handling the client is reassigned

18. A case record includes relevant social and psychological facts about the client, the nature of his request, his feeling about his situation, his attitude towards the agency and his use of and reaction to treatment.
    In addition, it should always contain

    A. routine history
    B. complete details of personality development and emotional relationships
    C. detailed process accounts of all contacts
    D. data necessary for understanding the problem and the factors important in arriving at a solution

19. The CHIEF basis for the inability of a troubled client to express his problem clearly to the investigator is that the client

    A. sees his problem in complex terms and does not think it possible to give the investigator the whole picture
    B. has erected defenses against emotions that seem to him inadmissible or intolerable
    C. cannot describe how he feels about his problem
    D. views the situation as unlikely to be solved and is blocked in self-expression

20. In aggressive casework, when an investigator visits a multi-problem family, he should begin by

    A. arranging individual interviews with the children
    B. outlining the steps to be taken in the solution of their problems

C. inviting the family to visit the agency so that a normal casework situation may be created
D. explaining what points of risk or danger exist in their situation and inviting an expression of their feelings

21. The job of the supervisory investigator may be considered in part an administrative one CHIEFLY because it

   A. requires administrative training or experience
   B. involves a direct relationship with the executive office of the department
   C. entails responsibility for staff development
   D. calls for planning, organizing, and coordinating

22. If a supervisory investigator discovers that the amount of the grant in a particular case is inaccurate, he should

   A. make the necessary adjustments and assign another investigator to the case
   B. caution all investigators in the unit to be more careful in the future
   C. assume that the investigator's computation was correct when it was made
   D. arrange to have the investigator review the budget with the client and make the necessary adjustments

23. If, in the process of investigating eligibility for assistance, discrepancies occur between the applicant's statement of his situation and that given by a relative interviewed, the investigator should USUALLY

   A. accept the relative's statement since the relative has less interest in falsifying the facts
   B. return to the client for clarification of the situation
   C. immediately discount the relative's statement since he may be motivated by his legal responsibility for supporting the applicant
   D. point out the discrepancies to the relative and ask him for any explanation he can give

24. In evaluating the adequacy of an individual's income, an investigator should place PRIMARY emphasis on

   A. its value in relation to the average income
   B. the source of the income
   C. its relation to the earning capacity of the individual
   D. its purchasing power

25. The length of residence required to make a person eligible for the various forms of public assistance available in the United States

   A. is the same in all states but is different among public assistance programs in a given state
   B. is the same in all states and among different public assistance programs in a given state
   C. is the same in all states for different categories
   D. varies among states and among different public assistance programs in a given state

KEY (CORRECT ANSWERS)

1. D
2. D
3. B
4. B
5. A

6. B
7. B
8. A
9. D
10. C

11. D
12. C
13. D
14. C
15. A

16. A
17. A
18. D
19. B
20. D

21. D
22. D
23. B
24. D
25. D

TEST 3

DIRECTIONS: Each question or incomplete statement is followed by several suggested answers or completions. Select the one that BEST answers the question or completes the statement. *PRINT THE LETTER OF THE CORRECT ANSWER IN THE SPACE AT THE RIGHT.*

1. A person who knowingly brings a needy person from another state into the state for the purpose of making him a public charge is guilty of

   A. violation of the Displaced Persons Act
   B. violation of the Mann Act
   C. a felony
   D. a misdemeanor

   1._____

2. An aged person who is unable to produce immediate proof of age has made an application for assistance. He states that it will take about a week to obtain the necessary proof and that he does not have enough money to provide meals for himself until then.
   If it appears that he is in immediate need, he should be told that

   A. temporary assistance will be provided pending the completion of the investigation
   B. a personal loan will be made to him from a revolving fund
   C. he should arrange for a small loan from private sources
   D. he will have to produce an affidavit witnessed by two relatives who will vouch for the accuracy of his statements before any assistance can be provided

   2._____

3. If the investigator learns during an interview that the client has applied for assistance without the knowledge of her husband, even though he is a member of the same household, the investigator should

   A. appear not to notice this oversight but watch for other evidences of marital discord
   B. make no mention of this to the applicant but, before taking final action, send a note to the husband asking him to come in
   C. discuss this situation with the client and help her recognize the value of her husband's participation in the application
   D. point out to the applicant the implications of her behavior and ask for an explanation of her motives

   3._____

4. Of the sources through which an agency can seek information about the family background and economic needs of a particular client, the MOST important consists of

   A. records and documents covering the client
   B. interviews with the client's relatives
   C. the client's own story
   D. direct contacts with former employers

   4._____

5. The one of the following sources of evidence which would be MOST likely to give information needed to verify residence is

   A. family affidavits
   B. medical and hospital bills
   C. an original birth certificate
   D. rental receipts

   5._____

6. Vital statistics are a resource used by investigators to

    A. help establish eligibility through verification of births, deaths, and marriages
    B. help establish eligibility through verification of divorce proceedings
    C. secure proof of unemployment and eligibility for unemployment compensation
    D. secure indices of the cost of living in the larger cities

7. Case records should be considered confidential in order to

    A. permit investigators to make objective, rather than subjective, comments
    B. prevent recipients from comparing amounts of assistance given to other recipients
    C. keep pertinent information from other investigators
    D. protect clients and their families

8. Because the investigator generally is not trained as a psychiatrist, he should, when encountering psychiatric problems in the performance of his departmental duties,

    A. ignore such problems because they are beyond the scope of his responsibilities
    B. inform the affected persons that he recognizes their problems personally but will take no official cognizance of them
    C. ask to be relieved of the cases in which these problems are met and recommend that they be assigned to a psychiatrist
    D. recognize such problems where they exist and make referrals to the proper sources for treatment

9. Inasmuch as periodic visits to clients at home are required by the department, according to good work practice, it is MOST desirable for the investigator to

    A. visit without appointment as this gives him a chance to see the person and the house *as they really are* and forestalls changing things to create a different impression
    B. write giving an appointment time as this saves the investigator from visiting when people are not at home and helps him to plan his work more efficiently
    C. write suggesting an appointment time so that the client may be prepared for the interview and the investigator uses his time economically
    D. advise all applicants during their first interview that they will be visited periodically but will not be given definite appointments

10. Assuming that careful interpretation has been given but an applicant for assistance refuses to accede to the necessary procedures to establish his eligibility, the MOST preferable of the following courses of action for the investigator to take would be to

    A. do nothing further
    B. grant a temporary delay in the hope that the applicant will change his mind
    C. try to ascertain why the applicant feels as he does, but to respect his decision if he refuses to change his mind
    D. proceed to check on all the facts possible even though the applicant has not given his permission

11. The PRIMARY purpose in discussing with an applicant the steps in determining his eligibility and the kind of verification of facts which the agency will need is to

    A. enable the applicant to understand the basis of eligibility and participate in determining it
    B. protect the position of the agency so that there will be no comeback if the application is not granted
    C. give the applicant an opportunity to modify any statement he may have made previously
    D. promote public relations for the agency since the applicant will tell others how the agency is operating

12. Of the following, the LEAST valid reason for the maintenance of the case record is to

    A. furnish reference material for other investigators
    B. improve the quality of service to the client
    C. show how the funds are being expended
    D. reduce the complexities of the case to manageable proportions

13. A public agency will lean more on forms than a private agency in the same field of activity because

    A. forms simplify the recording responsibilities of newly appointed investigators
    B. public records are of the family agency type
    C. the governmental framework requires a greater degree of standardization
    D. more interviews and visits are made in connection with public cases

14. In spite of the need which most of us have of finding rules and procedures to guide us, we must face the difficulty at the outset that there is no such thing as a model case record.
    Of the following, the BEST justification for this statement is that

    A. records should be written to suit the case
    B. case recording should be patterned after the best models obtainable
    C. rules cannot be applied to case work because each case requires individual treatment
    D. the establishment of routine and procedures in investigatory work is an ideal which cannot be realized

15. In attempting to discover whether an applicant for aid has had any previous experience as a recipient through other agencies in the community, the investigator should

    A. check the application with the social service exchange
    B. send the fingerprints of the applicant to the Police Department
    C. consult the latest records of the department
    D. ask the applicant to submit a notarized statement to the effect that such aid has not been received from any other source

16. Suppose a client whom you are investigating has borrowed $250 in order to purchase an evening gown for one of her children who is being graduated from high school. She is planning to repay the loan at the rate of ten dollars a week and presents verification of this transaction as well as the purchase.
    As an investigator, you would be complying with the BEST casework principles by

A. telling the client her grant will be reduced in view of her ability to manage on ten dollars less each week
B. telling the client that she must never do this again
C. explaining to the client how her action will make it more difficult for the family to get along on their limited grant
D. suggesting that she return the dress and repay the borrowed money in this way

17. An investigator determined, while investigating an applicant for Medical Assistance for the Aged, that the applicant's income and resources are over and above the limits permitted under the Medical Assistance for the Aged program. However, the applicant's medical needs seem to be extensive, and the applicant insists that he cannot pay for his needed medical care.
The investigator should

   A. accept the case for Medical Assistance for the Aged in the normal manner and await a determination of the cost of the medical care in order to determine if there is actually a budget deficit
   B. have the cost of the medical care determined prior to making any decision as to acceptance or rejection of the case
   C. handle the case exactly as he would the case of an applicant for any other type of assistance who does not have a budget deficit
   D. reject the case for Medical Assistance for the Aged until the applicant can obtain verification of the cost of his needed medical care

17.____

18. Of the following, the choice of method to be used in the supervisory process should be influenced MOST by the

   A. number and type of cases carried by each investigator
   B. emotional maturity of the investigator
   C. number of investigators supervised and their past experience
   D. subject matter to be learned and the long range goals of supervision

18.____

19. In an evaluation conference with an investigator, the BEST approach for the supervisor to take is to

   A. help the investigator to identify his strengths, as a basis for working on his weaknesses
   B. identify the investigator's weaknesses and help him overcome them
   C. allow the investigator to identify his weaknesses first and then suggest ways of overcoming them
   D. discuss the investigator's weaknesses but emphasize his strengths

19.____

20. Assume that an investigator is discouraged about the progress of his work and feels that it is futile to attempt to cope with many of his cases.
Of the following, it would be BEST for the supervisor to

   A. suggest to the investigator that such feelings are inappropriate for a professional worker
   B. tell the investigator that he must seek professional help in order to overcome these feelings
   C. reduce the investigator's caseload and give him cases that are less complex
   D. review with the investigator several of his cases in which there were obvious accomplishments

20.____

21. The supervisor is responsible for providing the investigator with the following means of support, with the EXCEPTION of

    A. interest and advice on his personal problems
    B. instruction on community resources
    C. inspiration for carrying out the work of the agency
    D. understanding his strengths and limitations

21.____

22. When an investigator frequently takes the initiative in asking questions and discussing problems during a supervisory conference, this is probably an indication that the

    A. supervisor is not sufficiently interested in the investigator
    B. conference is a positive learning experience for the investigator
    C. worker is hostile and resists supervision
    D. supervisor's position of authority is in question

22.____

23. When a supervisor finds that one of his investigators cannot accept criticism, of the following, it would be BEST for the supervisor to

    A. have the investigator transferred to another supervisor
    B. warn the investigator of disciplinary proceedings unless his attitude changes
    C. have the investigator suspended after explaining the reason
    D. explore with the investigator his attitude toward authority

23.____

24. Of the following, the condition which the inexperienced investigator is LEAST likely to be aware of, without the guidance of the supervisor, is

    A. when he is successful in helping a client
    B. when he is not making progress in helping a client
    C. that he has a personal bias toward certain clients
    D. that he feels insecure because of lack of experience

24.____

25. The supervisor should provide an inexperienced investigator with controls as well as freedom MAINLY because controls will

    A. enable him to set up his own controls sooner
    B. put him in a situation which is closer to the realities of life
    C. help him to use authority in handling a casework problem
    D. give him a feeling of security and lay the foundation for future self-direction

25.____

KEY (CORRECT ANSWERS)

1.	D	11.	A
2.	A	12.	D
3.	C	13.	C
4.	C	14.	A
5.	D	15.	A
6.	A	16.	C
7.	D	17.	A
8.	D	18.	D
9.	C	19.	A
10.	C	20.	D

21. A
22. B
23. D
24. C
25. D

EXAMINATION SECTION
TEST 1

DIRECTIONS: Each question or incomplete statement is followed by several suggested answers or completions. Select the one that BEST answers the question or completes the statement. *PRINT THE LETTER OF THE CORRECT ANSWER IN THE SPACE AT THE RIGHT.*

1. The one of the following which is the BEST description of a properly objective investigator is one who
    A. is friendly and sensitive to the client's feelings, without becoming emotionally involved
    B. is distant and impersonal, remaining unaffected by what the client says
    C. lets personal emotions enter as far as the client's situation calls for them
    D. becomes emotionally involved with the client's situation but without showing involvement

1.____

2. The one of the following which is MOST necessary for successfully interviewing a person who belongs to a culture different from that of the investigator is for the investigator to
    A. have some appreciation of the other culture
    B. ignore those cultural differences which lead to bias
    C. stay away from sensitive, touchy issues
    D. assume the mannerisms of people in the other culture

2.____

3. In fact-finding interviews, it is generally assumed that the smaller the number of interviewees, the greater the increase of reliability with the addition of others. The PROPER number of interviewees need to insure the accuracy of information obtain generally depends upon the
    A. educational level of those interviewed
    B. number of people who have the required information
    C. directness of the questions asked
    D. variability of the information received

3.____

4. The one of the following which is generally MOST likely to be accurately described in an interview by an interviewee is
    A. the presence of a large painting in the investigator's office
    B. the number of people in the investigator's waiting room
    C. space relations
    D. duration of time

4.____

5. The one of the following which is generally the BEST course of action for an investigator to take when interviewing a person who is reluctant to tell what he knows about a matter under investigation is to
    A. be curt and abrupt, and threaten the person with the consequences of his withholding information

5.____

B. be firm and severe, and pressure the person into telling the needed information
C. be patient and candid with the person being questioned about the investigation since doing otherwise is not ethical
D. give the person false information about the investigation so he will give the needed information without realizing its importance

6. It is often recommended that an investigator prepare in advance a list of questions or topics to be covered in an interview.
The MAIN reason for such a checklist is to
   A. allow investigations to be assigned to less efficient investigators
   B. eliminate a large amount of follow-up paperwork
   C. aid the investigator in remembering to cover all important documents
   D. aid the investigator in maintaining an objective distance from the person interviewed

7. Usually, the CHIEF advantage of a directive approach in an interview is that the
   A. investigator maintains control over the course of the interview
   B. person interviewed is more likely to be put at ease
   C. person interviewed is generally left free to direct the interview
   D. investigator will not suggest answers to the person interviewed

8. Usually, the CHIEF advantage of a non-directive approach by an investigator in conducting an interview is that the
   A. investigator generally conceals what he is looking for in the interview
   B. person interviewed is more likely to express his true feelings about the topic under discussion
   C. person interviewed is more likely to follow an idea introduced by the investigator
   D. investigator can keep the discussion limited to topics he believes to be relevant

9. The one of the following which is generally the LEAST likely to be accurate in a description of an event given to an investigator is a statement about
   A. the presence of an object
   B. the number of people, when their number is small
   C. locations of people
   D. duration of time

10. Assume that you, an investigator, are conducting a character investigation. In an interview, the one of the following character traits of the person being interviewed which can USUALLY be determined with a good degree of reliability is
    A. honesty   B. dependability
    C. forcefulness   D. perseverance

11. As an investigator, you have been assigned the task of obtaining a family's social history.
    The BEST place for you to interview members of the family while obtaining this social history would generally be in
    A. the family's home
    B. your agency's general offices
    C. the home of a friend of the family
    D. your own private office

12. You, an investigator, are checking someone's work history.
    The way for you to get the MOST reliable information from a previous employer is to
    A. send personal letters; the employer will respond to the personal attention
    B. send form letters; the employer will cooperate readily since little time or effort is asked of him
    C. arrange a personal interview; the employer may offer information he would not care to put in a letter or speak over the phone
    D. telephone; this method is as effective as a personal interview and is much more convenient

13. The effect that attestation, or the formal taking of an oath, has on witness testimony is to
    A. decrease accuracy, since a witness under oath is more nervous about what is said
    B. makes little difference, since the witness is not too swayed by an oath
    C. increase accuracy, since a witness under oath feels more responsibility for what is said
    D. eliminate inaccuracy unless there is deliberate perjury on the part of the witness

14. If an investigator obtains testimony from persons in interviews by means of interrogation or asking questions rather than by letting the person freely relate the testimony, what is said will GENERALLY be
    A. greater in range and less accurate
    B. greater in range and more accurate
    C. about the same in range and less accurate
    D. about the same in range and more accurate

15. Experienced investigators have learned to phrase their questions carefully in order to obtain the desired response.
    Of the following, the question which would usually elicit the MOST accurate answer is:
    A. "How old are you?"
    B. "What is your income?"
    C. "How are you today?"
    D. "What is your date of birth?"

16. The one of the following questions which would generally lead to the LEAST reliable answer is:
    A. "Did you see a wallet?"
    B. "Was the German Shepherd gray?"
    C. "Didn't you see the stop sign?"
    D. "Did you see the guard on duty?"

17. Some investigators may make a practice of observing details of the surroundings when interviewing in someone's home or office.
Such a practice is GENERALLY considered
    A. *undesirable*, mainly because such snooping is unwarranted, unethical invasion of privacy
    B. *undesirable*, mainly because useful information is rarely, if ever, gained this way
    C. *desirable*, mainly because useful insights into the character of the person interviewed may be gained
    D. *desirable*, mainly because it is impossible to evaluate a person adequately without such observation of his environment

18. The one of the following questions which MOST often lead to a reliable answer is:
    A. "Was his hair very dark?"
    B. "Wasn't there a clock on the wall?"
    C. "Was the automobile white or gray?"
    D. "Did you see a motorcycle?"

19. The one of the following which can MOST accurately be determined by an investigator by means of interviewing is
    A. a person's intelligence
    B. factual information about an event
    C. a person's aptitude for a specific task
    D. a person's perceptions of his own abilities

20. The one of the following which is MOST likely to help a person being interviewed feel at ease is for the investigator to
    A. let him start the conversation
    B. give him an abundance of time
    C. be relaxed himself
    D. open the interview by telling a joke

21. If the interviewee is to perceive some goal for himself in the interview and thus be motivated to participate in it, it is important that he clearly understands some of the aspects of the interview.
Of the following aspects, the one the interviewee needs LEAST to understand is
    A. the purpose of the interview
    B. the mechanics of interviewing
    C. the use made of the information he contributes
    D. what will be expected of him in the interview

22. As an investigator working on a project requiring inter-agency cooperation, you find that employees of an agency involved in the project are constantly making it difficult for you to obtain necessary information.
Of the following, the BEST action for you to take FIRST is to
    A. discuss the problem with your supervisor
    B. speak with your counterpart in the other agency

C. discuss the problem with the head of the uncooperative agency
D. contact the head of your agency

23. The investigator is justified in misleading the interviewee only when, in the investigator's judgment, this is clearly required by the problem being investigated.
Such a practice is
   A. *necessary*; there are times when complete honesty will impede a successful investigation
   B. *unnecessary*; such a tactic is unethical and should never be employed
   C. *necessary*; an investigator must be guided by success rather than ethical considerations in an investigation
   D. *unnecessary*; it is clearly doubtful whether such a practice will help the investigator conclude the investigation successfully

24. Assume that, in investigating a case of possible welfare fraud, it becomes necessary to hold an interview in the client's home in order to observe family interaction and conditions. Upon arriving, the investigator finds that the client's living room is noisy and crowded, with neighbors present and children running in and out.
Of the following, the BEST course of action for the investigator to take is to
   A. conduct the interview in the living room after telling the children to behave and asking the neighbors to leave
   B. tell the client that it is impossible to conduct the interview in the apartment and make an appointment for the next day in the investigators office
   C. suggest that they move from the living room into the kitchen where there is a table on which he can write
   D. try his best to conduct the interview in the noisy and crowded living room

25. You, an investigator, are giving testimony in court about a matter you have investigated. An attorney is questioning you in an abrasive, badgering way and, in an insulting manner, calls into doubt your ability as an investigator. You lose your temper and respond angrily, telling the attorney to stop harassing and insulting you.
Of the following, the BEST description of such a response is that it is generally
   A. *appropriate*; as a witness in court, you do not have to take insults from anybody, including an attorney
   B. *inappropriate*; losing your temper will show that you are weak and cannot be trusted as an investigator
   C. *appropriate*; a judge and jury will usually respect someone who responds strongly to unjust provocation
   D. *inappropriate*; such conduct is unprofessional and may unfavorably impress a judge and jury

KEY (CORRECT ANSWERS)

1.	A	11.	A
2.	A	12.	C
3.	D	13.	C
4.	A	14.	A
5.	C	15.	D
6.	C	16.	B
7.	A	17.	C
8.	B	18.	D
9.	D	19.	D
10.	C	20.	C

21.	B
22.	A
23.	A
24.	C
25.	D

TEST 2

DIRECTIONS: Each question or incomplete statement is followed by several suggested answers or completions. Select the one that BEST answers the question or completes the statement. *PRINT THE LETTER OF THE CORRECT ANSWER IN THE SPACE AT THE RIGHT.*

1. An investigator may have problems in obtaining information from persons who have a history of mental disturbance CHIEFLY because such persons are
   A. usually highly unstable so that they cannot give a coherent account of anything they have experienced
   B. usually very withdrawn so that they generally are unwilling to talk to anyone they do not know well
   C. often normal in manner so that an investigator may be unaware that their condition may bias information they provide
   D. often violent and may try to attack an investigator who questions them intensively about a topic which is sensitive

2. Empathy can be defined as the ability of one individual to respond sensitively and imaginatively to another's feelings.
   For an investigator to be empathetic during an interview is USUALLY
   A. *undesirable*, mainly because an investigator should never be influenced by the feelings of the one being interviewed
   B. *desirable*, mainly because an interview will not be productive unless the investigator takes the side of the person interviewed
   C. *undesirable*, mainly because empathy usually leads an investigator to be biased in favor of the person being interviewed
   D. *desirable*, mainly because this ability allows the investigator to direct his questions more effectively to the person interviewed

3. Assume that an investigator must, in the course of an investigation, question several people who know each other.
   To gather them all in one group and question them together is GENERALLY
   A. *good practice*, since any inaccurate information offered by one person would be corrected by others in the group
   B. *poor practice*, since people in a group rarely pay adequate attention to questions
   C. *good practice*, since the investigator will save much time and effort in this way
   D. *poor practice*, since the presence of several people can inhibit an individual from speaking

4. While conducting a character investigation of a potential employee, you, as an investigator, notice that most community members interviewed have negative opinions of the candidate.
   Of the following statements about the usefulness of community opinions in such a matter, the one which is LEAST accurate is that

A. prudence should be exercised in evaluating information received in a community contact
B. a community investigation sometimes elicits gossip which may present an exaggerated picture
C. community opinion is reliable when used to assess an individual's character
D. opinions which cannot be supported by facts must be considered as such

5. An effective investigator should know that the one of the following which LEAST describes why there is a wide range of individual behavior in human relations is that
   A. socio-economic status influences human behavior
   B. physical characteristics do not influence human behavior
   C. education influences human behavior
   D. childhood experience influences human behavior

5.____

6. In your investigative unit, you discern a growing friction between two co-workers which is beginning to impede the work of the unit.
Of the following, the approach you should FIRST adopt is to
   A. mediate the friction yourself; if unsuccessful, then inform your supervisor
   B. ignore the friction; although detrimental, it is beyond your authority to settle
   C. promptly discuss the friction and possible course of action with other members of your unit
   D. promptly inform your supervisor of the friction and let him handle the matter

6.____

7. In certain cases, in order that an investigation be conducted successfully, an investigator must have the cooperation of people in the community.
The one of the following which BEST describes how an investigator may gain community cooperation in an investigation is by
   A. using persuasion
   B. using authority
   C. spending many hours in the community
   D. being friendly with community leaders

7.____

8. During a field investigation, an investigator encounters an uncooperative interviewee.
Of the following, the FIRST thing the investigator should do in such a situation is to
   A. try various appeals to win the interviewee over to a cooperative attitude
   B. try to ascertain the reason for non-cooperation
   C. promise the interviewee that all data will be kept confidential
   D. alter his interviewing technique with the uncooperative interviewee

8.____

9. You, as an investigator, discover that an interviewee who was requested to bring with him specific documents for his initial employment interview has forgotten the documents.

9.____

Of the following, the BEST course of action to take is to
- A. give the person a reasonable amount of time to furnish the document
- B. tell the person you will let him know how much additional time he could receive
- C. mark the person disqualified for employment; he has failed to provide reasonably requested data on time
- D. mark the person provisionally qualified for employment; upon receipt of the documents, he will be permanently qualified

10. As an investigator checking interviewees' work experience, you realize that the person whom you are to interview is only marginally fluent in English and has, therefore, requested permission to bring a translator with him.
    Of the following, the BEST course of action is to inform the interviewee that
    - A. outside translators may not be used
    - B. only city translators may be used
    - C. state law requires fluency in English of all civil servants
    - D. he may be assisted in the interview by his translator

11. Assume that during the course of an interview, an investigator is verbally attacked by the person being interview.
    Of the following, it would be MOST advisable for the investigator to
    - A. answer back in a matter-of-fact manner
    - B. ask the person to apologize and discontinue the interview
    - C. ignore the attack but adjourn the interview to another day
    - D. use restraint and continue the interview

12. Assume that an investigator finds that the person he is interviewing has difficulty finishing his sentences and seems to be groping for words.
    In such a case, the BEST approach for the investigator to take is to
    - A. say what he thinks the person has in mind
    - B. proceed patiently without calling attention to the problem
    - C. ask the person why he finds it difficult to finish his sentence
    - D. interrupt the interview until the person feels more relaxed

13. The one of the following which BEST describes the effect of the sympathetic approach in interviewing on the interviewee is that it will
    - A. have no discernible effect on the interviewee
    - B. calm the interviewee
    - C. lead the interviewee to understate his problems
    - D. mislead the interviewee

14. The one of the following characteristics which is a PRIMARY requisite for a successful investigative interview is
    - A. total curiosity
    - B. total sympathy
    - C. complete attention
    - D. complete dedication

15. Assume that you, an investigator, become aware that one of your colleagues has a drinking problem which is affecting the operations of your unit.
    Of the following, the action which you should take FIRST is to
    A. give your colleague time to resolve the problem himself
    B. discuss the problem with your colleague
    C. inform your supervisor of the problem
    D. not involve yourself in your colleague's problem

16. Assume that an Assistant District Attorney has asked you, the investigator of an alleged welfare fraud, to conduct a follow-up interview with a primary state witness.
    The one of the following which is MOST important in arranging such an interview is to
    A. keep the witness cooperative
    B. conduct the matter in secret
    C. allow the witness to determine where and when the interview takes place
    D. conduct the interview as soon as possible to insure a strong case

17. Assume that an investigative unit has received a complex task requiring team work.
    Of the following, the one which is LEAST essential to the operations of a team effort is
    A. a small group
    B. a leader
    C. regular interaction between team members
    D. separate office space for each team member

18. By examining a candidate's employment record, an investigator can determine many things about the candidate.
    Of the following, the one which is LEAST apparent from an employment record is the candidate's
    A. character
    B. willingness to work
    C. capacity to get along with co-workers
    D. potential for advancing in civil service

19. Assume that you, an investigator, are conducting an investigative interview in which the person being interviewed is using the interview as a forum for venting his anti-civil service feelings.
    Of the following, the FIRST thing that you should do is to
    A. agree with the person; perhaps that will shorten the outburst
    B. respectfully disagree with the person; the decorum of the interview has already been disrupted
    C. courteously and objectively direct the interview to the relevant issue
    D. reschedule the interview to another mutually agreeable time

5 (#2)

20. The pattern of an investigative interview is LARGELY set by the   20.____
    A. person being interviewed
    B. person conducting the interview
    C. nature of the investigation
    D. policy of the agency employing the interviewer

21. Assume that a person being interviewed, who had been talking freely, suddenly   21.____
    tries to change the subject.
    To a trained interviewer, this behavior would mean that the person PROBABLY
    A. knew very little about the subject
    B. realized that he was telling too much
    C. decided that his privacy was being violated
    D. realized that he was becoming confused

22. Assume that you, an investigator, receive a telephone call from an unknown   22.____
    individual requesting information about a case you are currently investigating.
    In such a situation, the BEST course of action for you to take is to
    A. give him the information over the telephone
    B. tell him to write to your department for the information
    C. send him the information, retaining a copy for your files
    D. tell him to call back, giving you additional time to check into the matter

23. Assume that you, an investigator, are responding to a written query from a   23.____
    member of the public protesting a certain procedure employed by your agency.
    In such a case, your response should stress MOST the
    A. difficulty that a large agency encounters in trying to treat all members of
       the public fairly
    B. idea that the procedure in question will be discontinued if enough
       complaints are received
    C. necessity for the procedure
    D. origin of the procedure

Questions 24-25.

DIRECTIONS: Questions 24 and 25 are to be answered in the light of the information given in
            the following passage.

Assume that a certain agency is having a problem at one of its work locations because a sizable portion of the staff at that location is regularly tardy in reporting to work. The management of the agency is primarily concerned about eliminating the problem and is not yet too concerned about taking any disciplinary action. You are an investigator working for this agency, and though you have never had any contact with this location, you are assigned to investigate to determine, if possible, what might be causing this problem.

After several interviews, you see that low morale created by poor supervision at this location is at least part of the problem. Then, the last person you will interview before submitting your report tells you, when asked the reason for his tardiness, "*Well, I don't know; I just can't get up in the morning. So when I do get going, I've got to rush to get here. And just between you and me, I've lost interest in the job. Working conditions are bad, and it's hard for me to be enthusiastic about working here."*

24. Given the goals of the investigation and assuming that the investor was using a non-directive approach in this interview, of the following, the investigator's MOST effective response should be:
    A. "You know, you are building a bad record of tardiness."
    B. "Can you tell me more about this situation?"
    C. "What kind of person is your superior?"
    D. "Do you think you are acting fairly towards the agency by being late so often?"

25. Given the goals of the investigation and assuming the investigator was using a directed approach in this interview, of the following, the investigator's response should be
    A. "That doesn't seem like much of an excuse to me."
    B. "What do you mean by saying that you've lost interest?"
    C. What problems are there with the supervision you are getting?"
    D. "How do you think your tardiness looks in your personnel record?"

KEY (CORRECT ANSWERS)

1.	C		11.	D
2.	D		12.	B
3.	D		13.	B
4.	C		14.	C
5.	B		15.	C
6.	D		16.	A
7.	A		17.	D
8.	B		18.	D
9.	A		19.	C
10.	D		20.	B

21. B
22. B
23. C
24. B
25. C

EXAMINATION SECTION
TEST 1

DIRECTIONS: Each question or incomplete statement is followed by several suggested answers or completions. Select the one that BEST answers the question or completes the statement. *PRINT THE LETTER OF THE CORRECT ANSWER IN THE SPACE AT THE RIGHT.*

1. An investigator uses Forms A, B, and C in filling out his investigation reports. He uses Form B five times as often as Form A, and he uses Form C three times as often as Form B.
If the total number of all forms used by the investigator in a month equal 735, how many times was Form B used?
   A. 150 B. 175 C. 205 D. 235

2. Of all the investigators in one agency, 25% work in a particular building. Of these, 12% have desks on the 14th floor.
What percentage of the investigators work in this building but do NOT have desks on the 14th floor?
   A. 12% B. 13% C. 22% D. 23%

3. An investigator is given two reports to read. Report P is 160 pages long and takes the investigator 3 hours and 20 minutes to read.
If Report S is 254 pages long and the investigator reads it at the same rate as he reads Report P, how long will it take him to read Report S? _____ hours _____ minutes.
   A. 4; 15 B. 4; 50 C. 5; 10 D. 5; 30

4. A team of 6 investigators was assigned to interview 234 people.
If half the investigators conduct twice as many interviews as the other half, and the slow group interviews 12 persons a day, how many days would it take to complete this assignment? _____ days.
   A. 4½ B. 5 C. 6 D. 6½

5. The investigators in one agency conduct an average of 12 interviews an hour from 10 A.M. to 12 noon and from 1 P.M. to 5 P.M. daily. The director of his agency knows from past experience that 20% of those called in to be interviewed are unable to keep the appointments that were scheduled.
If the director wants his staff to be kept occupied with interviews for the entire time period that has been set aside for this function, how many appointments should be scheduled for each day?
   A. 86 B. 90 C. 96 D. 101

6. An investigator has a 430-page report to read. The first day, he is able to read 20 pages. The second day, he reads 10 pages more than the first day, and the third day, he reads 15 pages more than the second day.

1._____

2._____

3._____

4._____

5._____

6._____

If, on the following days, he continues to read at the same rate as he was reading on the third day, he will complete the report on the _____ day.
A. 7th B. 8th C. 10th D. 11th

7. The 36 investigators in an agency are each required to submit 25 investigation reports a week. These reports are filled out on a certain form, and only one copy of the form is needed per report.
Allowing 20% for waste, how many packages of 45 forms a piece should be ordered for each weekly period?
A. 15 B. 20 C. 25 D. 30

8. During the fiscal year, an investigative unit received $260 for stationery and telephone expenditures. It spent 43% for stationery and 1/3 of the balance for telephone service.
The amount of money that was left at the end of the fiscal year was MOST NEARLY
A. $49 B. $50 C. $99 D. $109

Questions 9-10.

DIRECTIONS: Questions 9 and 10 are to be answered SOLELY on the data given below.

Number of days absent per worker (sickness)	1	2	3	4	5	6	7	8 or Over
Number of Workers	96	45	16	3	1	0	1	0

Total Number of Workers: 500

9. The TOTAL number of man days lost due to illness in 2020 was
A. 137 B. 154 C. 162 D. 258

10. Of the 500 workers studied, the number who lost NO days due to sickness in 2020 was
A. 230 B. 298 C. 338 D. 372

Questions 11-13.

DIRECTIONS: Questions 11 through 13 are to be answered SOLELY on the basis of the following passage.

The rise of urban-industrial society has complicated the social arrangements needed to regulate contacts between people. As a consequence, there has been an unprecedented increase in the volume of laws and regulations designed to control individual conduct and to govern the relationship of the individual to others. In a century, there has been an eight-fold increase in the crimes for which one may be prosecuted.

For these offenses, the courts have the ultimate responsibility for redressing wrongs and convicting the guilty. The body of legal precepts gives the impression of an abstract and evenhanded dispensation of justice. Actually, the personnel of the agencies applying these precepts are faced with the difficulties of fitting abstract principles to highly variable situations emerging from the dynamics of everyday life. It is inevitable that discrepancies should exist between precept and practice.

The legal institutions serve as a framework for the social order by their slowness to respond to the caprices of transitory fad. This valuable contribution exacts a price in terms of the inflexibility of legal institutions in responding to new circumstances. This possibility is promoted by the changes in values and norms of the dynamic larger culture of which the legal precepts are a part.

11. According to the above passage, the increase in the number of laws and regulations during the twentieth century can be attributed to the
    A. complexity of modern industrial society
    B. increased seriousness of offenses committed
    C. growth of individualism
    D. anonymity of urban living

12. According to the above passage, which of the following presents a problem to the staff of legal agencies? The
    A. need to eliminate the discrepancy between precept and practice
    B. necessity to apply abstract legal precepts to rapidly changing conditions
    C. responsibility for reducing the number of abstract legal principles
    D. responsibility for understanding offenses in terms of the real-life situations from which they emerge

13. According to the above passage, it can be concluded that legal institutions affect social institutions by
    A. preventing change
    B. keeping pace with its norms and values
    C. changing its norms and values
    D. providing stability

Questions 14-16.

DIRECTIONS: Questions 14 through 16 are to be answered SOLELY on the basis of information given in the following passage.

A personnel interviewer, selecting job applicants, may find that he reacts badly to some people even on first contact. This reaction cannot usually be explained by things that the interviewee has done or said. Most of us have had the experience of liking or disliking, of feeling comfortable and uncomfortable with people on first acquaintance, long before we have had a chance to make a conscious, rational decision about them. Often, too, our liking or disliking is transmitted to the other person by subtle processes such as gestures, posture, voice intonations, or choice of words. The point to be kept in mind is this: the relations between people are complex and occur at several levels, from the conscious to the unconscious. This is true whether the relationship is brief or long, formal or informal.

Some of the major dynamics of personality which operate on the unconscious level are projection, sublimation, rationalization, and repression. Encountering these for the first time, one is apt to think of them as representing pathological states. In the extreme, they undoubtedly are, but they exist so universally that we must consider them also to be parts of normal personality.

Without necessarily subscribing to any of the numerous theories of personality, it is possible to describe personality in terms of certain important aspects or elements. We are all aware of ourselves as thinking organisms.

This aspect of personality, the conscious part, is important for understanding human behavior, but it is not enough. Many find it hard to accept the notion that each person also has an unconscious. The existence of the unconscious is no longer a matter of debate. It is not possible to estimate at all precisely what proportion of our total psychological life is conscious, what proportion unconscious. Everyone who has studied the problem, however, agrees that consciousness is the smaller part of personality. Most of what we are and do is a result of unconscious processes. To ignore this is to risk mistakes.

14. The above passage suggests that an interviewer can be MOST effective if he   14.____
    A. learns how to determine other peoples' unconscious motivations
    B. learns how to repress his own unconsciously motivated mannerisms and behavior
    C. can keep others from feeling that he either likes or dislikes them
    D. gains an understanding of how the unconscious operates in himself and in others

15. It may be inferred from the above passage that the *subtle processes*, such as   15.____
    gestures, posture, voice intonation, or choice of words referred to in the first paragraph are USUALLY
    A. in the complete control of an expert investigator
    B. the determining factors in the friendships a person establishes
    C. controlled by a person's unconscious
    D. not capable of being consciously controlled

16. The above passage implies that various different personality theories are   16.____
    USUALLY
    A. so numerous and different as to be valueless to an investigator
    B. in basic agreement about the importance of the unconscious
    C. understood by the investigator who strives to be effective
    D. in agreement that personality factors such as projection and repression are pathological

Questions 17-19.

DIRECTIONS: Questions 17 through 19 are to be answered SOLELY on the basis of information contained in the following passage.

No matter how well the interrogator adjusts himself to the witness and how precisely he induces the witness to describe his observations, mistakes still can be made. The mistakes made by an experienced interrogator may be comparatively few, but as far as the witness is concerned, his path is full of pitfalls. Modern "witness psychology" has shown that even the most honest and trustworthy witnesses are apt to make grave mistakes in good faith. It is, therefore, necessary that the interrogator get an idea of the weak links in the testimony in order to check up on them in the event that something appears to be strange or not quite satisfactory.

Unfortunately, modern witness psychology does not yet offer any means of directly testing the credibility of testimony. It lacks precision and method, in spite of worthwhile attempts on the part of learned men. At the same time, witness psychology, through the gathering of many experience concerning the weaknesses of human testimony, has been of invaluable service. It shows clearly that only evidence of a technical nature has absolute value as proof.

Testimony may be separated into the following stages: (1) perception; (2) observation; (3) mind fixation of the observed occurrences, in which fantasy, association of ideas, and personal judgment participate; (4) expression in oral or written form, where the testimony is transferred from one witness to another or to the interrogator. Each of these stages offers innumerable possibilities for the distortion of testimony.

17. The above passage indicates that having witnesses talk to each other before testifying is a practice which is GENERALLY
    A. *desirable*, since the witnesses will be able to correct each other's errors in observation before testimony
    B. *undesirable*, since the witnesses will collaborate on one story to tell the investigator
    C. *undesirable*, since one witness may distort his testimony because of what another witness may erroneously say
    D. *desirable*, since witnesses will become aware of discrepancies in their own testimony and can point out the discrepancies to the investigator

18. According to the above passage, the one of the following which would be the MOST reliable for use as evidence would be the testimony of a
    A. handwriting expert about a signature on a forged check
    B. trained police officer about the identity of a criminal
    C. laboratory technician about an accident he has observed
    D. psychologist who has interviewed any witness who relate conflicting stories

19. Concerning the validity of evidence, it is clear from the above passage that
    A. only evidence of a technical nature is at all valuable
    B. the testimony of witnesses is so flawed that it is usually valueless
    C. an investigator, by knowing modern witness psychology, will usually be able to perceive mistaken testimony
    D. an investigator ought to expect mistakes in even the most reliable witness testimony

Questions 20-21.

DIRECTIONS: Questions 20 and 21 are to be answered SOLELY on the basis of information given in the following passage.

Since we generally assure informants that what they say is confidential, we are not free to tell one informant what the other has told us. Even if the informant says, "*I don't care who knows it; tell anybody you want to,*" we find it wise to treat the interview as confidential. An interviewer who relates to some informants what other informants have told him is likely to stir up anxiety and suspicion. Of course, the interviewer may be able to tell an informant what he has heard without revealing the source of his information. This may be perfectly appropriate where a story has wide currency so that an informant cannot infer the source of the information. But if an event is not widely known, the mere mention of it may reveal to one informant what another informant has said about the situation. How can the data be cross-checked in these circumstances.

20. The above passage IMPLIES that the anxiety and suspicion an interviewer may arouse by telling what has been learned in other interviews is due to the
    A. lack of trust the person interviewed may have in the interviewer's honesty
    B. troublesome nature of the material which the interviewer has learned in other interviews
    C. fact that the person interviewed may not believe that permission was given to repeat the information
    D. fear of the person interviewed that what he is telling the interviewer will be repeated

21. The above passage is MOST likely part of a longer passage dealing with
    A. ways to verify data gathered in interviews
    B. the various anxieties a person being interviewed may feel
    C. the notion that people sometimes say things they do not mean
    D. ways an interview can avoid seeming suspicious

Questions 22-23.

DIRECTIONS: Questions 22 and 23 are to be answered SOLELY on the basis of information given below.

The ability to interview rests not on any single trait, but on a vast complex of them. Habits, skills, techniques, and attitudes are all involved. Competence in interviewing is acquired only after careful and diligent study, prolonged practice (preferably under supervision), and a good bit of trial and error; for interviewing is not an exact science; it is an art. Like many other arts, however, it can and must draw on science in several of its aspects.

There is always a place for individual initiative, for imaginative innovations, and for new combinations of old approaches. The skilled interviewer cannot be bound by a set of rules. Likewise, there is not a set of rules which can guarantee to the novice that his interviewing will be successful. There are, however, some accepted, general guideposts which may help the beginner to avoid mistakes, learn how to conserve this efforts, and establish effective working relationships with interviewees; to accomplish, in short, what he sets out to do.

22. According to the above passage, rules and standard techniques for interviewing are
    A. helpful for the beginner, but useless for the experienced, innovative interviewer
    B. destructive of the innovation and initiative needed for a good interviewer
    C. useful for even the experienced interviewer who may, however, sometimes go beyond them
    D. the means by which nearly anybody can become an effective interviewer

23. According to the above passage, the one of the following which is a prerequisite to competent interviewing is
    A. avoid mistakes
    B. study and practice
    C. imaginative innovation
    D. natural aptitude

Questions 24-27.

DIRECTIONS: Questions 24 through 27 are to be answered SOLELY on the basis of information given in the following passage.

The question of what material is relevant is not as simple as it might seem. Frequently, material which seems irrelevant to the inexperienced has, because of the common tendency to disguise and distort and misplace one's feelings, considerable significance. It may be necessary to let the client "ramble on" for a while in order to clear the decks, as it were, so that he may get down to things that really are on his mind. On the other hand, with an already disturbed person, it may be important for the interviewer to know when to discourage further elaboration of upsetting material. This is especially the case where the worker would be unable to do anything about it. An inexperienced interviewer might, for instance, be intrigued with the bizarre elaboration of material that the psychotic produces, but further elaboration of this might encourage the client in his instability. A too random discussion may indicate that the interviewee is not certain in what areas the interviewer is prepared to help him, and he may be seeking some direction. Or again, satisfying though it may be for the interviewer to have the interviewee tell him intimate details, such revelations sometimes need to be checked or encouraged only in small doses. An interviewee who has "talked too much" often reveals subsequent anxiety. This is illustrated by the fact that frequently after a "confessional" interview, the interviewee surprises the interviewer by being withdrawn, inarticulate, or hostile, or by breaking the next appointment.

24. Sometimes a client may reveal certain personal information to an interviewer and subsequently may feel anxious about this revelation.
    If, during an interview, a client begins to discuss very personal matters, it would be BEST to
    A. tell the client, in no uncertain terms, that you're not interested in personal details
    B. ignore the client at this point
    C. encourage the client to elaborate further on the details
    D. inform the client that the information seems to be very personal

25. The author indicates that clients with severe psychological disturbances pose an especially difficult problem for the inexperienced interviewer.
The difficulty lies in the possibility of the client
    A. becoming physically violent and harming the interviewer
    B. rambling on for a while
    C. revealing irrelevant details which may be followed by cancelled appointments
    D. reverting to an unstable state as a result of interview material

26. An interviewer should be constantly alert to the possibility of obtaining clues from the client as to the problem areas.
According to the above passage, a client who discusses topics at random may be
    A. unsure of what problems the interviewer can provide help with
    B. reluctant to discuss intimate details
    C. trying to impress the interviewer with his knowledge
    D. deciding what relevant material to elaborate on

27. The evaluation of a client's responses may reveal substantial information that may aid the interviewer in assessing the problem areas that are of concern to the client. Responses that seemed irrelevant at the time of the interview may be of significance because
    A. considerable significance is attached to all relevant material
    B. emotional feelings are frequently masked
    C. an initial *rambling on* is often a prelude to what is actually bothering the client
    D. disturbed clients often reveal subsequent anxiety

Questions 28-30.

DIRECTIONS: Questions 28 through 30 are to be answered SOLELY on the basis of the following passage.

The physical setting of the interview may determine its entire potentiality. Some degree of privacy and a comfortable relaxed atmosphere are important. The interviewee is not encouraged to give much more than his name and address if the interviewer seems busy with other things, if people are rushing about, if there are distracting noises. He has a right to feel that, whether the interview lasts five minutes or an hour, he has, for that time, the undivided attention of the interviewer. Interruptions, telephone calls, and so on, should be reduced to a minimum. If the interviewee has waited in a crowded room for what seems to him an interminably long period, he is naturally in mood to sit down and discuss what is on his mind. Indeed, by that time, the primary thing on his mind may be his irritation at being kept waiting, and he frequently feels it would be impolite to express this. If a wait or interruptions have been unavoidable, it is always helpful to give the client some recognition that these are disturbing and that we can naturally understand that they make it more difficult for him to proceed. At the same time, if he protests that they have not troubled him, the interviewer can best accept his statements at their face value, as further insistence that they must have been disturbing may be interpreted by him as accusing, and he may conclude that the interviewer has been personally hurt by his irritation.

28. Distraction during an interview may tend to limit the client's responses. In a case where an interruption has occurred, it would be BEST for the investigator to
    A. terminate this interview and have it rescheduled for another time period
    B. ignore the interruption since it is not continuous
    C. express his understanding that the distraction can cause the client to feel disturbed
    D. accept the client's protests that he has been troubled by the interruption

29. To maximize the rapport that can be established with the client, an appropriate physical setting is necessary. At the very least, some privacy would be necessary.
    In addition, the interviewer should
    A. always appear to be busy in order to impress the client
    B. focus his attention only on the client
    C. accept all the client's statements as being valid
    D. stress the importance of the interview to the client

30. Clients who have been waiting quite some time for their interview may, justifiably, become upset.
    However, a client may initially attempt to mask these feelings because he may
    A. personally hurt the interviewer
    B. want to be civil
    C. feel that the wait was unavoidable
    D. fear the consequences of his statement

KEY (CORRECT ANSWERS)

1.	B	11.	A	21.	A
2.	C	12.	B	22.	C
3.	D	13.	D	23.	B
4.	D	14.	D	24.	D
5.	B	15.	C	25.	D
6.	D	16.	B	26.	A
7.	C	17.	C	27.	B
8.	C	18.	A	28.	C
9.	D	19.	D	29.	B
10.	C	20.	D	30.	B

TEST 2

DIRECTIONS: Each question or incomplete statement is followed by several suggested answers or completions. Select the one that BEST answers the question or completes the statement. *PRINT THE LETTER OF THE CORRECT ANSWER IN THE SPACE AT THE RIGHT.*

Questions 1-5.

DIRECTIONS: In Questions 1 through 5, choose the statement which is BEST from the point of view of English usage suitable for a business report.

1.
   A. The client's receiving of public assistance checks at two different addresses were disclosed by the investigation.
   B. The investigation disclosed that the client was receiving public assistance checks at two different addresses.
   C. The client was found out by the investigator to be receiving public assistance checks at two different addresses.
   D. The client has been receiving public assistance checks at two different addresses, disclosed the investigation

   1.____

2.
   A. The investigation of complaints are usually handled by this unit, which deals with internal security problems in the department.
   B. This unit deals with internal security problems in the department; usually investigating complaints.
   C. Investigating complaints is this unit's job, being that it handles internal security problems in the department
   D. This unit deals with internal security problems in the department and usually investigates complaints.

   2.____

3.
   A. The delay in completing this investigation was caused by difficulty in obtaining the required documents from the candidate.
   B. Because of difficulty in obtaining the required documents from the candidate is the reason that there was a delay in completing this investigation.
   C. Having had difficulty in obtaining the required documents from the candidate, there was a delay in completing this investigation.
   D. Difficulty in obtaining the required documents from the candidate had the affect of delaying the completion of this investigation.

   3.____

4.
   A. This report, together with documents supporting our recommendation, are being submitted for your approval.
   B. Documents supporting our recommendation is being submitted with the report for your approval.
   C. This report, together with documents supporting our documentation, is being submitted for your approval.
   D. The report and documents supporting our recommendation is being submitted for your approval.

   4.____

84

5. A. Several people were interviewed and numerous letters were sent before this case was completed.
    B. Completing this case, interviewing several people and sending numerous letters were necessary.
    C. To complete this case needed interviewing several people and sending numerous letters.
    D. Interviewing several people and sending numerous letters was necessary to complete the case.

Questions 6-20.

DIRECTIONS: For each of the sentences numbered 6 to 20, select from the options given below the MOST applicable choice, and mark your answer accordingly.
A. The sentence is correct.
B. The sentence contains a spelling error only.
C. The sentence contains an English grammar error only.
D. The sentence contains both a spelling error and an English grammar error.

6. He is a very dependible person whom we expect will be an asset to this division.

7. An investigator often finds it necessary to be very diplomatic when conducting an interview.

8. Accurate detail is especially important if court action results from an investigation.

9. The report was signed by him and I since we conducted the investigation jointly.

10. Upon receipt of the complaint, an inquiry was begun.

11. An employee has to organize his time so that he can handle his workload efficiantly.

12. It was not apparent that anyone was living at the address given by the client.

13. According to regulations, there is to be at least three attempts made to locate the client.

14. Neither the inmate nor the correction officer was willing to sign a formal statement.

15. It is our opinion that one of the persons interviewed were lying.

16. We interviewed both clients and departmental personel in the course of this investigation.

17. It is concievable that further research might produce additional evidence.

18. There are too many occurences of this nature to ignore.

19. We cannot accede to the candidate's request. 19.____

20. The submission of overdue reports is the reason that there was a delay in completion of this investigation. 20.____

Questions 21-2.

DIRECTIONS: Each of Questions 21 through 25 consists of three sentences lettered A, B, and C. In each of these questions, one of the sentences may contain an error in grammar, sentence structure, or punctuation, or all three sentences may be correct. If one of the sentences in a question contains an error in grammar, sentence structure, or punctuation, print in the space at the right the capital letter preceding the sentence which contains the error. If all three sentences are correct, print the letter D.

21. A. Mr. Smith appears to be less competent than I in performing these duties. 21.____
    B. The supervisor spoke to the employee, who had made the error, but did not reprimand him.
    C. When he found the book lying on the table, he immediately notified the owner.

22. A. Being locked in the desk, we were certain that the papers would not be taken. 22.____
    B. It wasn't I who dictated the telegram; I believe it was Eleanor.
    C. You should interview whoever comes to the office today.

23. A. The clerk was instructed to set the machine on the table before summoning the manager. 23.____
    B. He said that he was not familiar with those kind of activities.
    C. A box of pencils, in addition to erasers and blotters, was included in the shipment.

24. A. The supervisor remarked, "Assigning an employee to the proper type of work is not always easy." 24.____
    B. The employer found that each of the applicants were qualified to perform the duties of the position.
    C. Any competent student is permitted to take this course if he obtains the consent of the instructor.

25. A. The prize was awarded to the employee whom the judges believed to be most deserving. 25.____
    B. Since the instructor believes this book is the better of the two, he is recommending it for use in the school.
    C. It was obvious to the employees that the completion of the task by the scheduled date would require their working overtime.

KEY (CORRECT ANSWERS)

1.	B	11.	B
2.	D	12.	B
3.	A	13.	C
4.	C	14.	A
5.	A	15.	C
6.	D	16.	B
7.	A	17.	B
8.	A	18.	B
9.	C	19.	A
10.	A	20.	C

21. B
22. A
23. B
24. B
25. D

EXAMINATION SECTION
TEST 1

DIRECTIONS: Each question or incomplete statement is followed by several suggested answers or completions. Select the one that BEST answers the question or completes the statement. *PRINT THE LETTER OF THE CORRECT ANSWER IN THE SPACE AT THE RIGHT.*

1. An interview is BEST conducted in private primarily because
   A. the person interviewed will tend to be less self-conscious
   B. the interviewer will be able to maintain his continuity of thought better
   C. it will insure that the interview is "off the record"
   D. people tend to "show off" before an audience

   1.____

2. An interviewer can BEST establish a good relationship with the person being interviewed by
   A. assuming casual interest in the statements made by the person being interviewed
   B. taking the point of view of the person interviewed
   C. controlling the interview to a major extent
   D. showing a genuine interest in the person

   2.____

3. An interviewer will be better able to understand the person interviewed and his problems if he recognizes that much of the person's behavior is due to motives
   A. which are deliberate   B. of which he is unaware
   C. which are inexplicable   D. which are kept under control

   3.____

4. An interviewer's attention must be directed toward himself as well as toward the person interviewed.
   This statement means that the interviewer should
   A. keep in mind the extent to which his own prejudices may influence his judgment
   B. rationalize the statements made by the person interviewed
   C. gain the respect and confidence of the person interviewed
   D. avoid being too impersonal

   4.____

5. More complete expression will be obtained from a person being interviewed if the interviewer can create the impression that
   A. the data secured will become part of a permanent record
   B. official information must be accurate in every detail
   C. it is the duty of the person interviewed to give accurate data
   D. the person interviewed is participating in a discussion of his own problems

   5.____

6. The practice of asking leading questions should be avoided in an interview because the
   A. interviewer risks revealing his attitudes to the person being interviewed
   B. interviewer may be led to ignore the objective attitudes of the person interviewed
   C. answers may be unwarrantedly influenced
   D. person interviewed will resent the attempt to lead him and will be less cooperative

7. A good technique for the interviewer to use in an effort to secure reliable data and to reduce the possibility of misunderstanding is to
   A. use casual undirected conversation, enabling the person being interviewed to talk about himself, and thus secure the desired information
   B. adopt the procedure of using direct questions regularly
   C. extract the desired information from the person being interviewed by putting him on the defensive
   D. explain to the person being interviewed the information desired and the reason for needing it

8. You are interviewing a patient to determine whether she is eligible for medical assistance. Of the many questions that you have to ask her, some are routine questions that patients tend to answer willingly and easily. Other questions are more personal and some patients tend to resent being asked them and avoid answering them directly.
   For you to begin the interview with the more personal questions would be
   A. *desirable*, because the end of the interview will go smoothly and the patient will be left with a warm feeling
   B. *undesirable*, because the patient might not know the answers to the questions
   C. *desirable*, because you will be able to return to these questions later to verify the accuracy of the responses
   D. *undesirable*, because you might antagonize the patient before you have had a chance to establish rapport

9. While interviewing a patient about her family composition, the patient asks you whether you are married.
   Of the following, the MOST appropriate way for you to handle this situation is to
   A. answer the question briefly and redirect her back to the topic under discussion
   B. refrain from answering the question and proceed with the interview
   C. advise the patient that it is more important that she answer your questions than that you answer hers, and proceed with the interview
   D. promise the patient that you will answer her question later, in the hope that she will forget, and redirect her back to the topic under discussion

10. In response to a question about his employment history, a patient you are interviewing rambles and talks about unrelated matters.
    Of the following, the MOST appropriate course of action for you to take FIRST is to

A. ask questions to direct the patient back to his employment history
B. advise him to concentrate on your questions and not to discuss irrelevant information
C. ask him why he is resisting a discussion of his employment history
D. advise him that if you cannot get the information you need, he will not be eligible for medical assistance

11. Suppose that a person you are interviewing becomes angry at some of the questions you have asked, calls you meddlesome and nosy, and states that she will not answer those questions.
Of the following, which is the BEST action for you to take?
    A. Explain the reasons the questions are asked and the importance of the answers
    B. Inform the interviewee that you are only doing your job and advise her that she should answer your questions or leave the office
    C. Report to your supervisor what the interviewee called you and refuse to continue the interview
    D. End the interview and tell the interviewee she will not be serviced by your department

12. Suppose that during the course of an interview the interviewee demands in a very rude way that she be permitted to talk to your supervisor or someone in charge.
Which of the following is probably the BEST way to handle this situation?
    A. Inform your supervisor of the demand and ask her to speak to the interviewee
    B. Pay no attention to the demands of the interviewee and continue the interview
    C. Report to your supervisor and tell her to get another interviewer for this interviewee
    D. Tell her you are the one "in charge" and that she should talk to you

13. Of the following, the outcome of an interview by an aide depends MOST heavily on the
    A. personality of the interviewee
    B. personality of the aide
    C. subject matter of the questions asked
    D. interaction between aide and interviewee

14. Some patients being interviewed are primarily interested in making a favorable impression.
The aide should be aware of the fact that such patients are more likely than other patients to
    A. try to anticipate the answers the interviewer is looking for
    B. answer all questions openly and frankly
    C. try to assume the role of interviewer
    D. be anxious to get the interview over as quickly as possible

15. The type of interview which an aide usually conducts is substantially different from most interviewing situations in all of the following aspects EXCEPT the
    A. setting
    B. kinds of clients
    C. techniques employed
    D. kinds of problems

16. During an interview, an aide uses a "leading question."
    This type of question is so-called because it generally
    A. starts a series of questions about one topic
    B. suggests the answer which the aide wants
    C. forms the basis for a following "trick" question
    D. sets, at the beginning, the tone of the interview

17. Casework interviewing is always directed to the client and his situation.
    The one of the following which is the MOST accurate statement with respect to the proper focus of an interview is that the
    A. caseworker limits the client to concentration on objective data
    B. client is generally permitted to talk about facts and feelings with no direction from the caseworker
    C. main focus in casework interviews is on feelings rather than facts
    D. caseworker is responsible for helping the client focus on any material which seems to be related to his problems or difficulties

18. Assume that you are conducting a training program for the caseworkers under your supervision. At one of the sessions, you discuss the problem of interviewing a dull and stupid client who gives a slow and disconnected case history.
    The BEST of the following interviewing methods for you to recommend in such a case in order to ascertain facts is for the caseworker to
    A. ask the client leading questions requiring "yes" or "no" answers
    B. request the client to limit his narration to the essential facts so that the interview can be kept as brief as possible
    C. review the story with the client, patiently asking simple questions
    D. tell the client that unless he is more cooperative he cannot be helped to solve his problem

19. A recent development in casework interviewing procedure, known as multiple-client interviewing, consists of interviews of the entire family at the same time. However, this may not be an effective casework method in certain situations. Of the following, the situation in which the standard individual interview would be preferable is when
    A. family member derive consistent and major gratification from assisting each other in their destructive responses
    B. there is a crucial family conflict to which the members are reacting
    C. the family is overwhelmed by interpersonal anxieties which have not been explored
    D. the worker wants to determine the pattern of family interaction to further his diagnostic understanding

20. A follow-up interview was arranged for an applicant in order that he could furnish 20._____
certain requested evidence. At this follow-up interview, the applicant still fails
to furnish the necessary evidence.
It would be MOST advisable for you to
   A. advise the applicant that he is now considered ineligible
   B. ask the applicant how soon he can get the necessary evidence and set a date for another interview
   C. question the applicant carefully and thoroughly to determine if he has misrepresented or falsified any information
   D. set a date for another interview and tell the applicant to get the necessary evidence by that time

KEY (CORRECT ANSWERS)

1.	A	11.	A
2.	D	12.	A
3.	B	13.	D
4.	A	14.	A
5.	D	15.	C
6.	C	16.	B
7.	D	17.	D
8.	D	18.	C
9.	A	19.	A
10.	A	20.	B

TEST 2

DIRECTIONS: Each question or incomplete statement is followed by several suggested answers or completions. Select the one that BEST answers the question or completes the statement. *PRINT THE LETTER OF THE CORRECT ANSWER IN THE SPACE AT THE RIGHT.*

1. In interviewing, the practice of anticipating an applicant's answers to questions is generally
   A. *desirable*, because it is effective and economical when it is necessary to interview large numbers of applicants
   B. *desirable*, because many applicants have language difficulties
   C. *undesirable*, because it is the inalienable right of every person to answer as he sees fit
   D. *undesirable*, because applicants may tend to agree with the answer proposed by the interviewer even when the answer is not entirely correct

   1._____

2. When an initial interview is being conducted, one way of starting is to explain the purpose of the interview to the applicant.
   The practice of starting the interview with such an explanation is generally
   A. *desirable*, because the applicant can then understand why the interview is necessary and what will be accomplished by it
   B. *desirable*, because it creates the rapport which is necessary to successful interviewing
   C. *undesirable*, because time will be saved by starting directly with the questions which must be asked
   D. *undesirable*, because the interviewer should have the choice of starting an interview in any manner he prefers

   2._____

3. For you to use responses such as "That's interesting," "Uh-huh," and "Good" during an interview with a patient is
   A. *desirable*, because they indicate that the investigator is attentive
   B. *undesirable*, because they are meaningless to the patient
   C. *desirable*, because the investigator is not supposed to talk excessively
   D. *undesirable*, because they tend to encourage the patient to speak freely

   3._____

4. During the course of a routine interview, the BEST tone of voice for an interviewer to use is
   A. authoritative   B. uncertain
   C. formal   D. conversational

   4._____

5. It is recommended that interviews which inquire into the personal background of an individual should be held in private.
   The BEST reason for this practice is that privacy
   A. allows the individual to talk freely about the details of his background
   B. induces contemplative thought on the part of the interviewed individual
   C. prevents any interruptions by departmental personnel during the interview
   D. most closely resembles the atmosphere of the individual's personal life

   5._____

6. Assume that you are interviewing a patient to determine whether he has any savings accounts.
   To obtain this information, the MOST effective way to phrase your question would be:
   A. "You don't have any savings, do you?"
   B. "At which bank do you have a savings account?"
   C. "Do you have a savings account?"
   D. "May I assume that you have a savings account?"

7. You are interviewing a patient who is not cooperating to the extent necessary to get all required information. Therefore, you decide to be more forceful in your approach.
   In this situation, such a course of action is
   A. *advisable*, because such a change in approach may help to increase the patient's participation
   B. *advisable*, because you will be using your authority more effectively
   C. *inadvisable*, because you will not be able to change this approach if it doesn't produce results
   D. *inadvisable*, because an aggressive approach generally reduces the validity of the interview

8. You have attempted to interview a patient on two separate occasions, and both attempts were unsuccessful. The patient has been totally uncooperative and you sense a personal hostility toward you.
   Of the following, the BEST way to handle this type of situation would be to
   A. speak to the patient in a courteous manner and ask him to explain exactly what he dislikes about you
   B. inform the patient that you will not allow personality conflicts to disrupt the interview
   C. make no further attempt to interview the patient and recommend that he be billed in full
   D. discuss the problem with your supervisor and suggest that another investigator be assigned to try to interview the patient

9. At the beginning of an interview, a patient with normal vision tells you that he is reluctant to discuss his finances. You realize that it will be necessary in this case to ask detailed questions about his net income.
   When you begin this line of questioning, of the following, the LEAST important aspect you should consider is your
   A. precise wording of the question   B. manner of questioning
   C. tone of voice   D. facial expressions

10. A caseworker under your supervision has been assigned the task of interviewing a man who is applying for foster home placement for his two children. The caseworker seeks your advice as to how to question this man, stating that she finds the applicant to be a timid and self-conscious person who seems torn between the necessity of having to answer the worker's questions truthfully and the effect he thinks his answers will have on his application.

Of the following, the BEST method for the caseworker to use in order to determine the essential facts in this case is to
- A. assure the applicant that he need not worry since the majority of applications for foster home placement are approved
- B. delay the applicant's narration of the facts important to the case until his embarrassment and fears have been overcome
- C. ignore the statements made by the applicant and obtain all the required information from his friends and relatives
- D. inform the applicant that all statements made by him will be verified and are subject to the law governing perjury

11. Assume that a worker is interviewing a boy in his assigned group in order to help him find a job.
    At the BEGINNING of the interview, the worker should
    - A. suggest a possible job for the youth
    - B. refer the youth to an employment agency
    - C. discuss the youth's work history and skills with him
    - D. refer the youth to the manpower and career development agency

12. As part of the investigation to locate an absent father, you make a field visit to interview one of the father's friends. Before beginning the interview, you identify yourself to the friend and show him your official identification.
    For you to do this is, generally,
    - A. *good practice*, because the friend will have proof that you are authorized to make such confidential investigations
    - B. *poor practice*, because the friend may not answer your questions when he knows why you are interviewing him
    - C. *good practice*, because your supervisor can confirm from the friend that you actually made the interview
    - D. *poor practice*, because the friend may warn the absent father that your agency is looking for him

13. You are interviewing a client in his home as part of your investigation of an anonymous complaint that he has been receiving Medicaid fraudulently.
    During the interview, the client frequently interrupts your questions to discuss the hardships of his life and the bitterness he feels about his medical condition.
    Of the following, the BEST way for you to deal with these discussions is to
    - A. cut them off abruptly, since the client is probably just trying to avoid answering your questions
    - B. listen patiently, since these discussions may be helpful to the client and may give you information for your investigation
    - C. remind the client that you are investigating a complaint against him and he must answer directly
    - D. seek to gain the client's confidence by discussing any personal or medical problems which you yourself may have

14. While interviewing an absent father to determine his ability to pay child support, you realize that his answers to some of your questions contradict his answers to other questions.
    Of the following, the BEST way for you to try to get accurate information from the father is to
    A. confront him with his contradictory answers and demand an explanation from him
    B. use your best judgment as to which of his answers are accurate and question him accordingly
    C. tell him that he has misunderstood your questions and that he must clarify his answers
    D. ask him the same questions in different words and follow up his answer with related questions

15. Assume that an applicant, obviously under a great deal of stress, talks continuously and rambles, making it difficult for you to determine the exact problem and her need.
    In order to make the interview more successful, it would be BEST for you to
    A. interrupt the applicant and ask her specific questions in order to get the information you need
    B. tell the applicant that her rambling may be a basic cause of her problem
    C. let the applicant continue talking as long as she wishes
    D. ask the applicant to get to the point because other people are waiting for you

16. A worker must be able to interview clients all day and still be able to listen and maintain interest.
    Of the following, it is MOST important for you to show interest in the client because, if you appear interested,
    A. the client is more likely to appreciate your professional status
    B. the client is more likely to disclose a greater amount of information
    C. the client is less likely to tell lie
    D. you are more likely to gain your supervisor's approval

17. When you are interviewing clients, it is important to notice and record how they say what they say—angrily, nervously, or with "body English"—because these signs may
    A. tell you that the client's words are the opposite of what the client feels and you may need to dig to find out what those feeling are
    B. be the prelude to violent behavior which no aide is prepared to handle
    C. show that the client does not really deserve serious consideration
    D. be important later should you be asked to defend what you did for the client

18. The patient you are interviewing is reticent and guarded in responding to your questions. He is not providing the information needed to complete his application for medical assistance.
    In this situation, the one of the following which is the MOST appropriate course of action for you to take FIRST is to

A. end the interview and ask him to contact you when he is ready to answer your questions
B. advise the patient that you cannot end the interview until he has provided all the information you need to complete the application
C. emphasize to the patient the importance of the questions and the need to answer them in order to complete the application
D. advise the patient that if he answers your questions the interview will be easier for both of you

19. At the end of an interview with a patient, he describes a problem he is having with his teenage son, who is often truant and may be using narcotics. The patient asks you for advice in handling his son.
Of the following, the MOST appropriate action for you to take is to
    A. make an appointment to see the patient and his son together
    B. give the patient a list of drug counseling programs to which he may refer his son
    C. suggest to the patient that his immediate concern should be his own hospitalization rather than his son's problem
    D. tell the patient that you are not qualified to assist him but will attempt to find out who can

20. A MOST appropriate condition in the use of direct questions to obtain personal data in an interview is that, whenever possible,
    A. the direct questions be used only as a means of encouraging the person interviewed to talk about himself
    B. provision be made for recording the information
    C. the direct questions be used only after all other methods have failed
    D. the person being interviewed understands the reason for requesting the information

19.____
20.____

KEY (CORRECT ANSWERS)

1.	D	11.	C
2.	A	12.	A
3.	A	13.	B
4.	D	14.	D
5.	A	15.	A
6.	B	16.	B
7.	A	17.	A
8.	D	18.	C
9.	A	19.	D
10.	B	20.	D

READING COMPREHENSION
UNDERSTANDING AND INTERPRETING WRITTEN MATERIAL

EXAMINATION SECTION
TEST 1

DIRECTIONS: Each question or incomplete statement is followed by several suggested answers or completions. Select the one that BEST answers the question or completes the statement. *PRINT THE LETTER OF THE CORRECT ANSWER IN THE SPACE AT THE RIGHT.*

Questions 1-2.

DIRECTIONS: Questions 1 and 2 are to be answered SOLELY on the basis of the following passage.

The new suburbia that is currently being built does not look much different from the old; there has, however, been an increase in the class and race polarization that has been developing between the suburbs and the cities for several generations now. The suburbs have become the home for an ever larger proportion of working-class, middle-class, and upper-class whites; the cities, for an even larger proportion of poor and non-white people. A great number of cities are 30 to 50 percent non-white in population, with more and larger ghettos than cities have ever had. Now, there is greater urban poverty on the one hand, and stronger suburban opposition to open housing and related policies to solve the cities' problems on the other hand. The urban crisis will worsen; and although there is no shortage of rational solutions, nothing much will be done about the crisis unless white America permits a radical change of public policy and undergoes a miraculous change of attitude towards its cities and their populations.

1. Which of the following statements is IMPLIED by the above passage? 1.____
   A. The percentage of non-whites in the suburbs is increasing.
   B. The policies of suburbanites have contributed to the seriousness of the urban crisis.
   C. The problems of the cities defy rational solutions.
   D. There has been a radical change in the appearance of both suburbia and the cities in the past few years.

2. Of the following, the title which BEST describes the passage's main theme is: 2.____
   A. THE NEW SUBURBIA
   B. URBAN POVERTY
   C. URBAN-SUBURBAN POLARIZATION
   D. WHY AMERICANS WANT TO LIVE IN THE SUBURBS

Questions 3-4.

DIRECTIONS: Questions 3 and 4 are to be answered selecting the BEST interpretation of the following paragraph.

One of the most familiar *type* dichotomies is Jung's introvert versus extrovert. Introverts are motivated by principles, extroverts by expediency; introverts are thinkers, extroverts are doers; and so on. Analysis of the way people react to principle versus expediency situations, however, has demonstrated that most people would have to be described as ambiverts (i.e., they exhibit both introverted and extroverted behavior depending upon the specific situation). Of course, some people behave in a more introverted way than others. A graphic representation of the number of persons exhibiting various degrees of such behavior along a continuum would approximate the familiar bell-shaped curve.

3. A. Extreme extroverts exhibit deviant behavior.
    B. The bell-shaped curve would indicate that there are slightly more introverts than extroverts.
    C. A continuum is used to determine whether a person is an introvert or an extrovert.
    D. There is really very little difference between an introvert, an extrovert, or an ambivert.

4. A. Extroverts are not thinkers, and introverts are not doers.
    B. Ambiverts *think* more than they *do*.
    C. Ambiverts outnumber introverts in the general society.
    D. Extroverts possess fewer principles than introverts.

5. The fundamental desires for food, shelter, family, and approval, and their accompanying instinctive forms of behavior, are among the most important forces in human life because they are essential to and directly connected with the preservation and the welfare of the individual as well as of the race.
   According to this statement,

    A. as long as human beings are permitted to act instinctively, they will act wisely
    B. the instinct for self-preservation makes the individual consider his own welfare rather than that of others
    C. racial and individual welfare depend upon the fundamental desires
    D. the preservation of the race demands that instinctive behavior be modified

6. The growth of our cities, the increasing tendency to move from one part of the country to another, the existence of people of different cultures in the neighborhood, have together made it more and more difficult to secure group recreation as part of informal family and neighborhood life.
   According to this statement,

    A. the breaking up of family and neighborhood ties discourages new family and neighborhood group recreation
    B. neighborhood recreation no longer forms a significant part of the larger community
    C. the growth of cities crowds out the development of all recreational activities
    D. the non-English-speaking people do not accept new activities easily

7. Sublimation consists in directing some inner urge, arising from a lower psychological level into some channel of interest on a higher psychological level. Pugnaciousness, for example, is directed into some athletic activity involving combat, such as football or boxing, where rules of fair play and the ethics of the game lift the destructive urge for combat into a constructive experience and offer opportunities for the development of character and personality.

According to this statement,

- A. the manner of self-expression may be directed into constructive activities
- B. athletic activities such as football and boxing are destructive of character
- C. all conscious behavior on high psychological levels indicates the process of sublimation
- D. the rules of fair play are inconsistent with pugnaciousness

Questions 8-9.

DIRECTIONS: Questions 8 and 9 are to be answered on the basis of the following passage.

Just why some individuals choose one way of adjusting to their difficulties and others choose other ways is not known. Yet what an individual does when he is thwarted remains a reasonably good key to the understanding of his personality. If his responses to thwart-ings are emotional explosions and irrational excuses, he is tending to live in an unreal world. He may need help to regain the world of reality, the cause-and-effect world recognized by generations of thinkers and scientists. Perhaps he needs encouragement to redouble his efforts. Perhaps, on the other hand, he is striving for the impossible and needs to substitute a worthwhile activity within the range of his abilities. It is the part of wisdom to learn the nature of the world and of oneself in relation to it and to meet each situation as intelligently and as adequately as one can.

8. The title that BEST expresses the idea of this paragraph is

    A. ADJUSTING TO LIFE
    B. ESCAPE FROM REALITY
    C. THE IMPORTANCE OF PERSONALITY
    D. EMOTIONAL CONTROL

9. The writer argues that all should

    A. substitute new activities for old
    B. redouble their efforts
    C. analyze their relation to the world
    D. seek encouragement from others

Questions 10-15.

DIRECTIONS: Questions 10 through 15 are to be answered SOLELY on the basis of the information given in the paragraph below.

The use of role-playing as a training technique was developed during the past decade by social scientists, particularly psychologists, who have been active in training experiments. Originally, this technique was applied by clinical psychologists who discovered that a patient appears to gain understanding of an emotionally disturbing situation when encouraged to act out roles in that situation. As applied in government and business organizations, the purpose of role-playing is to aid employees to understand certain work problems involving interpersonal relations and to enable observers to evaluate various reactions to them. Thus, for example, on the problem of handling grievances, two individuals from the group might be selected to act out extemporaneously the parts of subordinate and supervisor. When this situation is enacted by various pairs among the class and the techniques and results are discussed, the members of the group are presumed to reach conclusions about the most effective means of handling similar situations. Often the use of role reversal, where participants take parts different from their actual work roles, assists individuals to gain more insight into other people's problems and viewpoints. Although role-playing can be a rewarding training device, the trainer must be aware of his responsibilities. If this technique is to be successful, thorough briefing of both actors and observers as to the situation in question, the participants' roles, and what to look for, is essential.

10. The role-playing technique was FIRST used for the purpose of

    A. measuring the effectiveness of training programs
    B. training supervisors in business organizations
    C. treating emotionally disturbed patients
    D. handling employee grievances

11. When role-playing is used in private business as a training device, the CHIEF aim is to

    A. develop better relations between supervisor and subordinate in the handling of grievances
    B. come up with a solution to a specific problem that has arisen
    C. determine the training needs of the group
    D. increase employee understanding of the human relation factors in work situations

12. From the above passage, it is MOST reasonable to conclude that when role-playing is used, it is preferable to have the roles acted out by

    A. only one set of actors
    B. no more than two sets of actors
    C. several different sets of actors
    D. the trainer or trainers of the group

13. Based on the above passage, a trainer using the technique of role reversal in a problem of first-line supervision should assign a senior enforcement agent to play the part of a(n)

    A. enforcement agent
    B. senior enforcement agent
    C. principal enforcement agent
    D. angry citizen

14. It can be inferred from the above passage that a *limitation* of role-play as a training method is that

    A. many work situations do not lend themselves to role-play
    B. employees are not experienced enough as actors to play the roles realistically
    C. only trainers who have psychological training can use it successfully
    D. participants who are observing and not acting do not benefit from it

15. To obtain good results from the use of role-play in training, a trainer should give participants

    A. a minimum of information about the situation so that they can act spontaneously
    B. scripts which illustrate the best method for handling the situation
    C. a complete explanation of the problem and the roles to be acted out
    D. a summary of work problems which involve interpersonal relations

Questions 16-20.

DIRECTIONS: Questions 16 through 20 are to be answered SOLELY on the basis of the following passage.

The dynamics of group behavior may be summed up by saying that the individuals in a group respond to many lines of force arising out of their relationship with every other member of a group and with the group itself. In addition, each member of a group quite naturally brings with him all the things that have been *bugging* him. Then, the situation or the setting in which the group meets, as well as the circumstances related to the formation of the group, are active working forces exerting some X influence upon each member of the group. Lastly, all of this kinetic energy is at the control of the person seeking to lead the group into some kind of action. If he is to produce something meaningful with the members of a group, he must utilize this energy, contain it, dissipate it in some fashion, or be faced with difficulty.

This dynamic force inherent in any group can be harnessed by a supervisor with leadership qualities, but it must be controlled. It will not be contained by acting without consultation with group members, by refusing to accept suggestions coming from the group, or by refusing to explain or even give notice of contemplated actions. However, it can be controlled by placing the focus upon the members of the group, rather than upon the supervisor, and depending upon the leader-supervisor to provide as many participative experiences for group members as is commensurate with his own decision-making responsibilities. It is true that this is subordinate-centered leadership, but the supervisor can gain strength through permissive leadership without sacrificing basic responsibilities for effective planning and adequate control of operations.

16. Of the following titles, the one that MOST closely describes the reading selection is

   A. THE SUPERVISOR WITH DYNAMIC LEADERSHIP POTENTIAL
   B. DISSIPATION OF GROUP ENERGY
   C. CONTROLLING GROUP RELATIONSHIPS
   D. SACRIFICING BASIC RESPONSIBILITIES

17. According to the above passage, the setting in which the group meets

   A. can readily be modified either in whole or in part
   B. must be made meaningful in some fashion to foster skills development
   C. can provide the sole source of group dynamics
   D. is one of the forces exerting influence on group members

18. According to the above passage, the members of the group

   A. should control their formation and development
   B. should control the circumstances of their meeting
   C. are influenced by the forces creating the group
   D. dissipate meaningless energy

19. According to the above passage, the effective group leader

   A. controls the focus of the group
   B. focuses his control over the group
   C. controls group forces by focusing upon group members
   D. focuses the group's forces upon himself

20. According to the above passage, effective leadership consists in
    A. partially compromising decision-making responsibilities
    B. partially sacrificing some basic responsibilities
    C. sometimes cultivating permissive subordinates
    D. providing participation for members of the group consistent with decision-making imperatives

Questions 21-22.

DIRECTIONS: Questions 21 and 22 are to be answered SOLELY on the basis of the following passage.

This country was built on the puritanical belief that honest toil was the foundation of moral rectitude, the cement of society, and the uphill road to progress. Idleness was sin. As a result, we treat free time today as a conditional joy. We permit outselves to relax only as a reward for hard work or as the recreation needed to put us back into shape for the job. Thus, the aimless delightful play of children gives way in adult life to a serious dedication to golf, the game that is so good for business.

21. According to the above passage, during former times in this country respectable work was considered to be MOST NEARLY a
    A. way to improve health
    B. form of recreation
    C. developer of good character
    D. reward for leisure

22. According to the point of view presented in the above passage, it would be MOST reasonable to assume that an employer would consider an employee's vacation to be a time for the employee to
    A. determine his own leisure time priorities
    B. loaf and relax
    C. learn new recreational skills
    D. increase his effectiveness at work

Questions 23-24.

DIRECTIONS: Questions 23 and 24 are to be answered SOLELY on the basis of the following passage.

A recent study revealed some very concrete evidence concerning the relationship between avocations and mental health. A number of well-adjusted persons were surveyed as to the type, number, and duration of their hobbies. The findings were compared to those from a similar survey of mentally disturbed persons. In the well-adjusted group, both the number of hobbies and the intensity with which they were pursued were far greater than that of the mentally disturbed group.

23. According to the above passage, the study showed that
    A. well-adjusted people engage in hobbies more widely and deeply than do mentally disturbed people
    B. hobbies, if taken seriously, serve to keep most people mentally well
    C. mental patients should be taught hobbies as a part of their therapy
    D. the degree of interest in hobbies plays an important role in maintaining good mental health

24. In reference to the study mentioned in the above passage, it is MOST accurate to say that it appears to have
    A. been based on a carefully-structured, complex research design
    B. considered the variables of mental health and hobby involvement
    C. contained a general definition of mental health
    D. given evidence of a causal relationship between hobbies and mental health

25. Across the years, our social sense has decreed that every position of social leadership, every place of influence, every concentration of social power in the hands of an individual, every instrument or agency that has aggregated to itself the power to affect the common welfare, has become by that very fact a social trust that must be administered for the common good. In our moral world, the social obligations of power are real and unescapable. On the basis of this statement, it would be MOST correct to state that
    A. an individual engaged in private enterprise does not have the social responsibility of one who holds public office
    B. social leadership carries with it the obligation to administer for the public good
    C. in our moral world, the abuse of the power is real and unescapable
    D. social leadership depends upon the aggregation of power in the hands of an individual or in an agency that wields concentrated influence

KEY (CORRECT ANSWERS)

1.	B	11.	D
2.	C	12.	C
3.	A	13.	A
4.	C	14.	A
5.	C	15.	C
6.	A	16.	C
7.	A	17.	D
8.	A	18.	C
9.	C	19.	C
10.	C	20.	D

21. C
22. D
23. A
24. B
25. B

TEST 2

DIRECTIONS: Each question or incomplete statement is followed by several suggested answers or completions. Select the one that BEST answers the question or completes the statement. *PRINT THE LETTER OF THE CORRECT ANSWER IN THE SPACE AT THE RIGHT.*

Questions 1-9.

DIRECTIONS: Questions 1 through 9 are to be answered SOLELY on the basis of the following passage.

The establishment of a procedure whereby the client's rent is paid directly by the Social Service agency has been suggested recently by many people in the Social Service field. It is believed that such a procedure would be advantageous to both the agency and the client. Under the current system, clients often complain that their rent allowances are not for the correct amount. Agencies, in turn, have had to cope with irate landlords who complain that they are not receiving rent checks until much later than their due date.

The proposed new system would involve direct payment of the client's rent by the agency to the landlord. Clients would not receive a monthly rent allowance. Under one possible implementation of such a system, special rent payment offices would be set up in each borough and staffed by Social Service clerical personnel. Each office would handle all work involved in sending out monthly rent payments. Each client would receive monthly notification from the Social Service agency that his rent has been paid. A rent office would be established for every three Social Service centers in each borough. Only in cases where the rental exceeds $350 per month would payment be made and records kept by the Social Service center itself rather than a special rent office. However, clients would continue to make all direct contacts through the Social Service center.

Files in the rent offices would be organized on the basis of client rental. All cases involving monthly rents up to, but not exceeding, $300 would be placed in salmon-colored folders. Cases with rents from $300 to $500 would be placed in buff folders, and those with rents exceeding $500, but less than $750 would be filed in blue folders. If a client's rental changed, he would be required to notify the center as soon as possible so that this information could be brought up-to-date in his folder and the color of his folder changed if necessary. Included in the information needed, in addition to the amount of rent, are the size of the apartment, the type of heat, and the number of flights of stairs to climb if there is no elevator.

Discussion as to whether the same information should be required of clients residing in city projects was resolved with the decision that the identical system of filing and updating of files should apply to such project tenants. The basic problem that might arise from the institution of such a program is that clients would resent being unable to pay their own rent. However, it is likely that such resentment would be only a temporary reaction to change and would disappear after the new system became standard procedure. It has been suggested that this program first be experimented with on a small scale to determine what problems may arise and how the program can be best implemented.

1. According to the above passage, there a number of complaints about the current system of rent payments. Which of the following is a complaint expressed in the passage?   1._____

107

A. Landlords complain that clients sometimes pay the wrong amount for their rent.
B. Landlords complain that clients sometimes do not pay their rent on time.
C. Clients say that the Social Service agency sometimes does not mail the rent out on time.
D. Landlords say that they sometimes fail to receive a check for the rent.

2. Assume that there are 15 Social Service centers in Manhattan.
According to the above passage, the number of rent offices that should be established in that borough under the new system is

A. 1 B. 3 C. 5 D. 15

3. According to the above passage, a client under the new system would receive

A. a rent receipt from the landlord indicating that Social Services has paid the rent
B. nothing since his rent has been paid by Social Services
C. verification from the landlord that the rent was paid
D. notices of rent payment from the Social Service agency

4. According to the above passage, a case record involving a client whose rent has changed from $310 to $540 per month should be changed from a _____ folder to a _____ folder.

A. blue; salmon-colored   B. buff; blue
C. salmon-colored; blue   D. yellow; buff

5. According to the above passage, if a client's rental is lowered because of violations in his building, he would be required to notify the

A. building department   B. landlord
C. rent payment office   D. Social Service center

6. Which one of the following kinds of information about a rented apartment is NOT mentioned in the above passage as being necessary to include in the client's folder?
The

A. floor number, if in an apartment house with an elevator
B. rental, if in a city project apartment
C. size of the apartment, if in a two-family house
D. type of heat, if in a city project apartment

7. Assume that the rent payment proposal discussed in the above passage is approved and ready for implementation in the city.
Which of the following actions is MOST in accordance with the proposal described in the above passage?

A. Change over completely and quickly to the new system to avoid the confusion of having clients under both systems.
B. Establish rent payment offices in all of the existing Social Service centers.
C. Establish one small rent payment office in Manhattan for about six months.
D. Set up an office in each borough and discontinue issuing rent allowances.

8. According to the above passage, it can be inferred that the MOST important drawback of the new system would be that once a program is started clients might feel

A. they have less independence than they had before
B. unable to cope with problems that mature people should be able to handle
C. too far removed from Social Service personnel to successfully adapt to the new requirements
D. too independent to work with the system

9. The above passage suggests that the proposed rent program be started as a pilot program rather than be instituted immediately throughout the city.
Of the following possible reasons for a pilot program, the one which is stated in the above passage as the MOST direct reason is that

A. any change made would then be only on a temporary basis
B. difficulties should be determined from small-scale implementation
C. implementation on a wide scale is extremely difficult
D. many clients might resent the new system

Questions 10-14.

DIRECTIONS: Questions 10 through 14 are to be answered SOLELY on the basis of the following passage.

PROCEDURE TO OBTAIN REIMBURSEMENT FROM DEPARTMENT OF HEALTH
FOR CARE OF PHYSICALLY HANDICAPPED CHILDREN

Application for reimbursement must be received by the Department of Health within 30 days of the date of hospital admission in order that the Department of Hospitals may be reimbursed from the date of admission. Upon determination that patient is physically handicapped, as defined under Chapter 780 of the State Laws, the ward clerk shall prepare seven copies of Department of Health Form A-1 or A-2, Application and Authorization, and shall submit six copies to the institutional Collections Unit. The ward clerk shall also initiate two copies of Department of Health Form B-1 or B-2, Financial and Social Report, and shall forward them to the institutional Collections Unit for completion of Page 1 and routing to the Social Service Division for completion of the Social Summary on Page 2. Social Service Division shall return Form B-1 or B-2 to the institutional Collections Unit which shall forward one copy of Form B-1 or B-2 and six copies of Form A-1 or A-2 to Central Office Division of Collections for transmission to Bureau of Handicapped Children, Department of Health.

10. According to the above paragraph, the Department of Health will pay for hospital care for

A. children who are physically handicapped
B. any children who are ward patients
C. physically handicapped adults and children
D. thirty days for eligible children

11. According to the procedure described in the above paragraph, the definition of what constitutes a physical handicap is made by the

A. attending physician
B. laws of the State
C. Social Service Division
D. ward clerk

12. According to the above paragraph, Form B-1 or B-2 is

    A. a three page form containing detachable pages
    B. an authorization form issued by the Department of Hospitals
    C. completed by the ward clerk after the Social Summary has been entered
    D. sent to the institutional Collections Unit by the Social Service Division

13. According to the above paragraph, after their return by the Social Service Division, the institutional Collections Unit keeps

    A. one copy of Form A-1 or A-2
    B. one copy of Form A-1 or A-2 and one copy of Form B-1 or B-2
    C. one copy of Form B-1 or B-2
    D. no copies of Forms A-1 or A-2 or B-1 or B-2

14. According to the above paragraph, forwarding the *Application and Authorization* to the Department of Health is the responsibility of the

    A. Bureau for Handicapped Children
    B. Central Office Division of Collections
    C. Institutional Collections Unit
    D. Social Service Division

Questions 15-19.

DIRECTIONS: Questions 15 through 19 are to be answered SOLELY on the basis of the following *total annual income adjustment* rules for household income.

The basic annual income is to be calculated by multiplying the total of the current weekly salaries of all adults (age 21 or over) by 52.

Upward and downward adjustments must be made to the basic annual salary to arrive at the *total adjusted annual income* for the household.

UPWARD ADJUSTMENTS

1. Add one-half of total overtime payments in the previous two years.
2. Add that part of the earnings of any minor in the household that exceeded $3,000 in the previous 12 months.

DOWNWARD ADJUSTMENTS

1. Deduct one-third of all educational tuition payments for household members in the previous 12 months.
2. Deduct the expense of going to and from work in excess of $30 per week per household member. This adjustment is made on the basis of the previous 12 months and should be computed for each household member individually for each week in which excess travel expenses were incurred.
3. Deduct that part of child care expenses which exceeded $1,500 in the previous 12 months.

15. In Household A, the husband has a weekly salary of $585 and the wife has just had her salary increased from $390 to $420 per week. In the previous 12 months, each had a paid continuous vacation of four weeks; the husband had to travel to a secondary work location every fourth week. His travel costs during those weeks were $42 per week. In the previous 12 months, they had child care costs of $1,470.
What is the TOTAL annual adjusted income for the household?

    A. $52,116   B. $52,104   C. $51,828   D. $51,234

15.____

16. In Household B, the husband has a weekly salary of $540. In the past year, he received overtime payments of $255. In the year before that, he received overtime payments of $1,221. His wife has just begun a job with a weekly salary of $330. As a result of this, annual child care expenses will be $2,130.
What is the TOTAL annual adjusted income for the household?

    A. $45,240   B. $45,348   C. $45,978   D. $46,824

16.____

17. In Household C, the husband has a weekly salary of $555. The wife has a weekly salary of $390. They each had expenses of $33 per week when traveling to and from work in the previous 12 months. The husband had an annual paid vacation of five weeks, and the wife had an annual paid vacation of three weeks in the previous year. There is a daughter in college for whom annual tuition payments of $1,710 were made in the previous 12 months.
What is the TOTAL annual adjusted income for the household?

    A. $48,258   B. $48,282   C. $49,140   D. $50,022

17.____

18. In Household D, the husband has a weekly salary of $465, the wife has a weekly salary of $330, and an adult daughter has a weekly salary of $285. The husband received overtime payments of $1,890 in the past year. In the year before that, he received no overtime payments. In the past year, there were weekly child care expenses of $210 per week for 47 weeks.
What is the TOTAL adjusted annual income for the household?

    A. $57,105   B. $48,735   C. $47,235   D. $46,845

18.____

19. In Household E, the husband has a weekly salary of $615. The wife has a weekly salary of $195. During the past year, there were tuition payments of $255 per month for 10 months per year for children in grade school and annual tuition payments of $2,310 for a boy in high school. What is the TOTAL adjusted annual income for the household?

    A. $39,570   B. $39,690   C. $40,500   D. $42,120

19.____

Questions 20-22.

DIRECTIONS: Questions 20 through 22 are to be answered SOLELY on the basis of the following paragraph.

Effective December 1, 2004, tenants thereafter admitted to public housing projects shall pay rents in accordance with Schedule DV if they are veterans of the Gulf War, and in accordance with Schedule D if they are not Gulf War veterans. However, all recipients of public assistance shall pay rents in accordance with Schedule DW. Tenants of public housing projects prior to the effective date of this change will continue to pay rent in accordance with Schedule C2 if they are veterans of the Iraqi War or the Gulf War, in accordance with

Schedule C if they are not such veterans, and in accordance with Schedule CW if they receive public assistance and if they are not eligible to use the C2 Schedule. In addition, effective December 1, 2004, when a tenant is accepted for assistance by the Department of Welfare, if such acceptance requires that the tenant pay a new rental as outlined above, the effective date of the new rental is to be the first of the month following the date that the tenant is accepted for assistance by the Department of Welfare instead of the first of the month following the date of application for public assistance.

20. John Jones, a Gulf War veteran, has been living in a public housing project since June 2003. He applied for public assistance on November 15, 2004 and was accepted for public assistance on December 17, 2004.
    If he continues to receive public assistance, his present rent should be based on the _____ Schedule.

    A. C2   B. CW   C. DV   D. DW

21. Jack Smith, who is not a veteran, moves into a public housing project in January 2006. If it should become necessary for him to apply for public assistance on February 10, 2006 and should he be accepted for such assistance on March 5, 2006, the rent that he pays in March 2006 should be based on the _____ Schedule.

    A. C   B. CW   C. D   D. DW

22. John Doe, a veteran of the Iraqi War, was admitted to a public housing project in August 2004. He applied for public assistance on February 1, 2005 and was accepted for such assistance on March 1, 2005.
    On April 1, 2005, his rent should

    A. change to the C2 Schedule
    B. remain on the C2 Schedule, as previously
    C. change to the CW Schedule
    D. remain on the CW Schedule, as previously

Questions 23-25.

DIRECTIONS: Questions 23 through 25 are to be answered SOLELY on the basis of the following paragraph.

It has been proposed that an act be passed to provide for family allowances in the form of cash payments, normally to mothers, for children under sixteen years of age. Allowances are supposed to be spent exclusively for the care and education of the children; otherwise, they may be discontinued. They would vary in amount according to the age of the child and would be conditional upon satisfactory school attendance and accomplishment. The allowance would be paid to all families, regardless of means, but income tax exemptions for dependents would be reduced in consequence. The act would also permit the withdrawal of children from school and their entrance into the labor market after completing eighth grade. However, there would be no financial advantage in sending a child to work since the allowances would approximate the child's net earnings. Proponents of this proposal claim as advantages that it would provide social justice by taking into account elements of family need not possible under any normal wage structure system, be simple to administer, encourage an increase in the birth rate, remove unwilling or incapable students from our middle schools, and provide financial aid to poor, large families without the stigma of public welfare.

23. According to the proposal, the one of the following factors which would be LEAST likely to cause a variation in the amount of the allowance to a family or cause a discontinuance of it is 23._____

    A. a change in family wealth
    B. poor school attendance record of a child
    C. a child's being left back
    D. use of the allowance money on a hobby of one of the parents

24. The LEAST accurate of the following statements concerning schooling under this proposal is: 24._____

    A. A 14-year-old girl attending the 6th grade of elementary school will not be permitted to leave school, even though her school work is unsatisfactory.
    B. A poor family will be encouraged to continue the schooling of their 15-year-old twins who are in the junior year of high school.
    C. A 14-year-old boy who has been graduated from elementary school, but whose school attendance has been unsatisfactory, will not be permitted to attend high school.
    D. The family of a 17-year-old high school senior who is an honor student will not receive an allowance.

25. College attendance of bright children of poor families may be aided by this proposal because 25._____

    A. such children will be assured of higher marks
    B. families are likely to be smaller and consequently parents will be better able to send their children to college
    C. more scholarships are likely to be offered by private colleges as a result of this proposal
    D. the financial subsidy granted for a child under 16 may help the family save money towards a college education

KEY (CORRECT ANSWERS)

1.	B	11.	B
2.	C	12.	D
3.	D	13.	C
4.	B	14.	B
5.	D	15.	A
6.	A	16.	C
7.	C	17.	B
8.	A	18.	B
9.	B	19.	C
10.	A	20.	A

21. C
22. B
23. A
24. C
25. D

———

PREPARING WRITTEN MATERIAL
EXAMINATION SECTION
TEST 1

DIRECTIONS: Each of Questions 1 through 5 consists of a sentence which may or may not be an example of good formal English usage. Examine each sentence, considering grammar, punctuation, spelling, capitalization, and awkwardness. Then choose the correct statement about it from the four options below it. If the English usage in the sentence given is better than any of the changes suggested in options B, C, or D, pick option A. (Do not pick an option that will change the meaning of the sentence.) *PRINT THE LETTER OF THE CORRECT ANSWER IN THE SPACE AT THE RIGHT.*

1. I don't know who could possibly of broken it. 1._____
   A. This is an example of good formal English usage.
   B. The word "who" should be replaced by the word "whom."
   C. The word "of" should be replaced by the word "have."
   D. The word "broken" should be replaced by the word "broke."

2. Telephoning is easier than to write. 2._____
   A. This is an example of good formal English usage.
   B. The word "telephoning" should be spelled "telephoneing."
   C. The word "than" should be replaced by the word "then."
   D. The words "to write" should be replaced by the word "writing."

3. The two operators who have been assigned to these consoles are on vacation. 3._____
   A. This is an example of good formal English usage.
   B. A comma should be placed after the word "operators."
   C. The word "who" should be replaced by the word "whom."
   D. The word "are" should be replaced by the word "is."

4. You were suppose to teach me how to operate a plugboard. 4._____
   A. This is an example of good formal English usage.
   B. The word "were" should be replaced by the word "was."
   C. The word "suppose" should be replaced by the word "supposed."
   D. The word "teach" should be replaced by the word "learn."

5. If you had taken my advice; you would have spoken with him. 5._____
   A. This is an example of good formal English usage.
   B. The word "advice" should be spelled "advise."
   C. The words "had taken" should be replaced by the word "take."
   D. The semicolon should be changed to a comma.

KEY (CORRECT ANSWERS)

1. C
2. D
3. A
4. C
5. D

TEST 2

DIRECTIONS: Select the correct answer. *PRINT THE LETTER OF THE CORRECT ANSWER IN THE SPACE AT THE RIGHT.*

1. The one of the following sentences which is MOST acceptable from the viewpoint of correct grammatical usage is:
   A. I do not know which action will have worser results.
   B. He should of known better.
   C. Both the officer on the scene, and his immediate supervisor, is charged with the responsibility.
   D. An officer must have initiative because his supervisor will not always be available to answer questions.

   1.____

2. The one of the following sentences which is MOST acceptable from the viewpoint of correct grammatical usage is:
   A. Of all the officers available, the better one for the job will be picked.
   B. Strict orders were given to all the officers, except he.
   C. Study of the law will enable you to perform your duties more efficiently.
   D. It seems to me that you was wrong in failing to search the two men.

   2.____

3. The one of the following sentences which does NOT contain a misspelled word is:
   A. The duties you will perform are similar to the duties of a patrolman.
   B. Officers must be constantly alert to sieze the initiative.
   C. Officers in this organization are not entitled to special privileges.
   D. Any changes in procedure will be announced publically.

   3.____

4. The one of the following sentences which does NOT contain a misspelled word is:
   A. It will be to your advantage to keep your firearm in good working condition.
   B. There are approximately fourty men on sick leave.
   C. Your first duty will be to pursuade the person to obey the law.
   D. Fires often begin in flameable material kept in lockers.

   4.____

5. The one of the following sentences which does NOT contain a misspelled word is:
   A. Offices are not required to perform technical maintainance.
   B. He violated the regulations on two occasions.
   C. Every employee will be held responable for errors.
   D. This was his nineth absence in a year.

   5.____

KEY (CORRECT ANSWERS)

1. D
2. C
3. C
4. A
5. B

TEST 3

DIRECTIONS: Select the correct answer. *PRINT THE LETTER OF THE CORRECT ANSWER IN THE SPACE AT THE RIGHT.*

1. You are answering a letter that was written on the letterhead of the ABC Company and signed by James H. Wood, Treasurer.
   What is usually considered to be the correct salutation to use in your reply?
   A. Dear ABC Company:
   B. Dear Sirs:
   C. Dear Mr. Wood:
   D. Dear Mr. Treasurer:

   1.____

2. Assume that one of your duties is to handle routine letters of inquiry from the public.
   The one of the following which is usually considered to be MOST desirable in replying to such a letter is a
   A. detailed answer handwritten on the original letter of inquiry
   B. phone call, since you can cover details more easily over the phone than in a letter
   C. short letter giving the specific information requested
   D. long letter discussing all possible aspects of the question raised

   2.____

3. The CHIEF reason for dividing a letter into paragraphs is to
   A. make the message clear to the reader by starting a new paragraph for each new topic
   B. make a short letter occupy as much of the page as possible
   C. keep the reader's attention by providing a pause from time to time
   D. make the letter look neat and businesslike

   3.____

4. Your superior has asked you to send an e-mail from your agency to a government agency in another city. He has written out the message and has indicated the name of the government agency.
   When you dictate the message to your secretary, which of the following items that your superior has NOT mentioned must you be sure to include?
   A. Today's date
   B. The full address of the government agency
   C. A polite opening such as "Dear Sirs"
   D. A final sentence such as "We would appreciate hearing from your agency in reply as soon as is convenient for you"

   4.____

5. The one of the following sentences which is grammatically preferable to the others is:
   A. Our engineers will go over your blueprints so that you may have no problems in construction.
   B. For a long time he had been arguing that we, not he, are to blame for the confusion.
   C. I worked on this automobile for two hours and still cannot find out what is wrong with it.
   D. Accustomed to all kinds of hardships, fatigue seldom bothers veteran policemen.

   5.____

KEY (CORRECT ANSWERS)

1. C
2. C
3. A
4. B
5. A

TEST 4

DIRECTIONS: Select the correct answer. *PRINT THE LETTER OF THE CORRECT ANSWER IN THE SPACE AT THE RIGHT.*

1. Suppose that an applicant for a job as snow laborer presents a letter from a former employer stating: "John Smith has a pleasing manner and never got into an argument with his fellow employees. He was never late or absent."
This letter
   A. indicates that with some training Smith will make a good snow gang boss
   B. presents no definite evidence of Smith's ability to do snow work
   C. proves definitely that Smith has never done any snow work before
   D. proves definitely that Smith will do better than average work as a snow laborer

   1.____

2. Suppose you must write a letter to a local organization in your section refusing a request in connection with collection of their refuse.
You should start the letter by
   A. explaining in detail the consideration you gave the request
   B. praising the organization for its service to the community
   C. quoting the regulation which forbids granting the request
   D. stating your regret that the request cannot be granted

   2.____

3. Suppose a citizen writes in for information as to whether or not he may sweep refuse into the gutter. A Sanitation officer answers as follows:
Dear Sir:
   No person is permitted to litter, sweep, throw or cast, or direct, suffer or permit any person under his control to litter, sweep, throw or cast any ashes, garbage, paper, dust, or other rubbish or refuse into any public street or place, vacant lot, air shaft, areaway, backyard or court.
                              Very truly yours,
                              John Doe
This letter is *poorly* written CHIEFLY because
   A. the opening is not indented   B. the thought is not clear
   C. the tone is too formal and cold D. there are too many commas used

   3.____

4. A section of a disciplinary report written by a Sanitation officer states: "It is requested that subject Sanitation man be advised that his future activities be directed towards reducing his recurrent tardiness else disciplinary action will be initiated which may result in summary discharge."
This section of the report is *poorly* written MAINLY because
   A. at least one word is misspelled   B. it is not simply expressed
   C. more than one idea is expressed   D. the purpose is not stated

   4.____

5. A section of a disciplinary report written by an officer states: "He comes in late. He takes too much time for lunch. He is lazy. I recommend his services be dispensed with."
This section of the report is *poorly* written MAINLY because
   A. it ends with a preposition   B. it is not well organized
   C. no supporting facts are stated   D. the sentences are too simple

   5.____

KEY (CORRECT ANSWERS)

1. B
2. D
3. C
4. B
5. C

PREPARING WRITTEN MATERIAL

PARAGRAPH REARRANGEMENT
COMMENTARY

The sentences that follow are in scrambled order. You are to rearrange them in proper order and indicate the letter choice containing the correct answer at the space at the right.

Each group of sentences in this section is actually a paragraph presented in scrambled order. Each sentence in the group has a place in that paragraph; no sentence is to be left out. You are to read each group of sentences and decide upon the best order in which to put the sentences so as to form a well-organized paragraph.

The questions in this section measure the ability to solve a problem when all the facts relevant to its solution are not given.

More specifically, certain positions of responsibility and authority require the employee to discover connection between events sometimes, apparently, unrelated. In order to do this, the employee will find it necessary to correctly infer that unspecified events have probably occurred or are likely to occur. This ability becomes especially important when action must be taken on incomplete information.

Accordingly, these questions require competitors to choose among several suggested alternatives, each of which presents a different sequential arrangement of the events. Competitors must choose the MOST logical of the suggested sequences.

In order to do so, they may be required to draw on general knowledge to infer missing concepts or events that are essential to sequencing the given events. Competitors should be careful to infer only what is essential to the sequence. The plausibility of the wrong alternatives will always require the inclusion of unlikely events or of additional chains of events which are NOT essential to sequencing the given events.

It's very important to remember that you are looking for the best of the four possible choices, and that the best choice of all may not even be one of the answers you're given to choose from.

There is no one right way to solve these problems. Many people have found it helpful to first write out the order of the sentences, as they would have arranged them, on their scrap paper before looking at the possible answers. If their optimum answer is there, this can save them some time. If it isn't, this method can still give insight into solving the problem. Others find it most helpful to just go through each of the possible choices, contrasting each as they go along. You should use whatever method feels comfortable and works for you.

While most of these types of questions are not that difficult, we've added a higher percentage of the difficult type, just to give you more practice. Usually there are only one or two questions on this section that contain such subtle distinctions that you're unable to answer confidently. And you then may find yourself stuck deciding between two possible choices, neither of which you're sure about.

EXAMINATION SECTION
TEST 1

DIRECTIONS: The sentences that follow are in scrambled order. You are to rearrange them in proper order and indicate the letter choice containing the correct answer. *PRINT THE LETTER OF THE CORRECT ANSWER IN THE SPACE AT THE RIGHT.*

1. Below are four statements labeled W, X, Y and Z.
   W. He was a strict and fanatic drillmaster.
   X. The word is always used in a derogatory sense and generally shows resentment and anger on the part of the user.
   Y. It is from the name of this Frenchman that we derive our English word, martinet.
   Z. Jean Martinet was the Inspector-General of Infantry during the reign of King Louis XIV.
   The PROPER order in which these sentences should be placed in a paragraph is:
   A. X, Z, W, Y   B. X, Z, Y, W   C. Z, W, Y, X   D. Z, Y, W, X

1.____

2. In the following paragraph, the sentences, which are numbered, have been jumbled.
   I. Since then it has undergone changes.
   II. It was incorporated in 1955 under the laws of the State of New York.
   III. Its primary purposes, a cleaner city, has, however, remained the same.
   IV. The Citizens Committee works in cooperation with the Mayor's Inter-departmental Committee for a Clean City.
   The order in which these sentences should be arranged to form a well-organized paragraph is:
   A. II, IV, I, III   B. III, IV, I, II   C. IV, II, I, III   D. IV, III, II, I

2.____

3.____

Questions 3-5.

DIRECTIONS: The sentences listed below are part of a meaningful paragraph but they are not given in their proper order. You are to decide what would be the BEST order in which to put the sentences so as to form a well-organized paragraph. Each sentence has a place in the paragraph; there are no extra sentences. You are then to answer Questions 3 through 5 inclusive on the basis of your rearrangements of these scrambled sentences into a properly organized paragraph.

In 1887 some insurance companies organized an Inspection Department to advise their clients on all phases of fire prevention and protection. Probably this has been due to the smaller annual fire losses in Great Britain than in the United States. It tests various fire prevention devices and appliances and determines manufacturing hazards and their safeguards. Fire research began earlier in the United States and is more advanced than in Great Britain. Later they established a laboratory specializing in electrical, mechanical, hydraulic, and chemical fields.

3. When the five sentences are arranged in proper order, the paragraph starts with the sentence which begins
   A. "In 1887…"   B. "Probably this…"   C. "It tests…"
   D. "Fire research…"   E. "Later they…"

4. In the last sentence listed above, "they" refers to
   A. the insurance companies
   B. the United States and Great Britain
   C. the Inspection Department
   D. clients
   E. technicians

5. When the above paragraph is properly arranged, it ends with the words
   A. "…and protection."
   B. "…the United States."
   C. "…their safeguards."
   D. "…in Great Britain."
   E. "…chemical fields."

KEY (CORRECT ANSWERS)

1. C
2. C
3. D
4. A
5. C

TEST 2

DIRECTIONS: In each of the questions numbered I through V, several sentences are given. For each question, choose as your answer the group of number that represents the MOST logical order of these sentences if they were arranged in paragraph form. *PRINT THE LETTER OF THE CORRECT ANSWER IN THE SPACE AT THE RIGHT.*

1.
   I. It is established when one shows that the landlord has prevented the tenant's enjoyment of his interest in the property leased.
   II. Constructive eviction is the result of a breach of the covenant of quiet enjoyment implied in all leases.
   III. In some parts of the United States, it is not complete until the tenant vacates within a reasonable time.
   IV. Generally, the acts must be of such serious and permanent character as to deny the tenant the enjoyment of his possessing rights.
   V. In this event, upon abandonment of the premises, the tenant's liability for that ceases.
   The CORRECT answer is:
   A. II, I, IV, III, V
   B. V, II, III, I, IV
   C. IV, III, I, II, V
   D. I, III, V, IV, II

2.
   I. The powerlessness before private and public authorities that is the typical experience of the slum tenant is reminiscent of the situation of blue-collar workers all through the nineteenth century.
   II. Similarly, in recent years, this chapter of history has been reopened by anti-poverty groups which have attempted to organize slum tenants to enable them to bargain collectively with their landlords about the conditions of their tenancies.
   III. It is familiar history that many of the worker remedied their condition by joining together and presenting their demands collectively.
   IV. Like the workers, tenants are forced by the conditions of modern life into substantial dependence on these who possess great political aid and economic power.
   V. What's more, the very fact of dependence coupled with an absence of education and self-confidence makes them hesitant and unable to stand up for what they need from those in power.
   The CORRECT answer is:
   A. V, IV, I, II, III
   B. II, III, I, V, IV
   C. III, I, V, IV, II
   D. I, IV, V, III, II

3.
   I. A railroad, for example, when not acting as a common carrier may contract away responsibility for its own negligence.
   II. As to a landlord, however, no decision has been found relating to the legal effect of a clause shifting the statutory duty of repair to the tenant.
   III. The courts have not passed on the validity of clauses relieving the landlord of this duty and liability.
   IV. They have, however, upheld the validity of exculpatory clauses in other types of contracts.

V. Housing regulations impose a duty upon the landlord to maintain leased premises in safe condition.
VI. As another example, a bailee may limit his liability except for gross negligence, willful acts, or fraud.

The CORRECT answer is:
A. II, I, VI, IV, III, V
B. I, III, IV, V, VI, II
C. III, V, I, IV, II, VI
D. V, III, IV, I, VI, II

4.
I. Since there are only samples in the building, retail or consumer sales are generally eschewed by mart occupants, and in some instances, rigid controls are maintained to limit entrance to the mart only to those persons engaged in retailing.
II. Since World War I, in many larger cities, there has developed a new type of property, called the mart building.
III. It can, therefore, be used by wholesalers and jobbers for the display of sample merchandise.
IV. This type of building is most frequently a multi-storied, finished interior property which is a cross between a retail arcade and a loft building.
V. This limitation enables the mart occupants to ship the orders from another location after the retailer or dealer makes his selection from the samples.

The CORRECT answer is:
A. II, IV, III, I, V
B. IV, III, V, I, II
C. I, III, II, IV, V
D. I, IV, II, III, V

5.
I. In general, staff-line friction reduces the distinctive contribution of staff personnel.
II. The conflicts, however, introduce an uncontrolled element into the managerial system.
III. On the other hand, the natural resistance of the line to staff innovations probably usefully restrains over-eager efforts to apply untested procedures on a large scale.
IV. Under such conditions, it is difficult to know when valuable ideas are being sacrificed.
V. The relatively weak position of staff, requiring accommodation to the line, tends to restrict their ability to engage in free, experimental innovation.

The CORRECT answer is:
A. IV, II, III, I, V
B. I, V, III, II, IV
C. V, III, I, II, IV
D. II, I, IV, V, III

KEY (CORRECT ANSWERS)

1. A
2. D
3. D
4. A
5. B

TEST 3

DIRECTIONS: Questions 1 through 4 consist of six sentences which can be arranged in a logical sequence. For each question, select the choice which places the numbered sentences in the MOST logical sequent. *PRINT THE LETTER OF THE CORRECT ANSWER IN THE SPACE AT THE RIGHT.*

1.
   I. The burden of proof as to each issue is determined before trial and remains upon the same party throughout the trial.
   II. The jury is at liberty to believe one witness' testimony as against a number of contradictory witnesses.
   III. In a civil case, the party bearing the burden of proof is required to prove his contention by a fair preponderance of the evidence.
   IV. However, it must be noted that a fair preponderance of evidence does not necessarily mean a greater number of witnesses.
   V. The burden of proof is the burden which rests upon one of the parties to an action to persuade the trier of the facts, generally the jury, that a proposition he asserts is true.
   VI. If the evidence is equally balanced, or if it leaves the jury in such doubt as to be unable to decide the controversy either way, judgment must be given against the party upon whom the burden of proof rests.
   The CORRECT answer is:
   A. III, II, V, IV, I, VI
   B. I, II, VI, V, III, IV
   C. III, IV, V, I, II, VI
   D. V, I, III, VI, IV, II

2.
   I. If a parent is without assets and is unemployed, he cannot be convicted of the crime of non-support of a child.
   II. The term "sufficient ability" has been held to mean sufficient financial ability.
   III. It does not matter if his unemployment is by choice or unavoidable circumstances.
   IV. If he fails to take any steps at all, he may be liable to prosecution for endangering the welfare of a child.
   V. Under the penal law, a parent is responsible for the support of his minor child only if the parent is "of sufficient ability."
   VI. An indigent parent may meet his obligation by borrowing money or by seeking aid under the provisions of the Social Welfare Law.
   The CORRECT answer is:
   A. VI, I, V, III, II, IV
   B. I, III, V, II, IV, VI
   C. V, II, I, III, VI, IV
   D. I, VI, IV, V, II, III

3.
   I. Consider, for example, the case of a rabble rouser who urges a group of twenty people to go out and break the windows of a nearby factory.
   II. Therefore, the law fills the indicated gap with the crime of inciting to riot.
   III. A person is considered guilty of inciting to riot when he urges ten or more persons to engage in tumultuous and violent conduct of a kind likely to create public alarm.
   IV. However, if he has not obtained the cooperation of at least four people, he cannot be charged with unlawful assembly.

129

V. The charge of inciting to riot was added to the law to cover types of conduct which cannot be classified as either the crime of "riot" or the crime of "unlawful assembly."
VI. If he acquires the acquiescence of at least four of them, he is guilty of unlawful assembly even if the project does not materialize.

The CORRECT answer is:
A. III, V, I, VI, IV, II
B. V, I, IV, VI, II, III
C. III, IV, I, V, II, VI
D. V, I, IV, VI, III, II

4.
I. If, however, the rebuttal evidence presents an issue of credibility, it is for the jury to determine whether the presumption has, in fact, been destroyed.
II. Once sufficient evidence to the contrary is introduced, the presumption disappears from the trial.
III. The effect of a presumption is to place the burden upon the adversary to come forward with evidence to rebut the presumption.
IV. When a presumption is overcome and ceases to exist in the case, the fact or facts which gave rise to the presumption still remain.
V. Whether a presumption has been overcome is ordinarily a question for the court.
VI. Such information may furnish a basis for a logical inference.

The CORRECT answer is:
A. IV, VI, II, V, I, III
B. III, II, V, I, IV, VI
C. V, III, VI, IV, II, I
D. V, IV, I, II, VI, III

KEY (CORRECT ANSWERS)

1. D
2. C
3. A
4. B

ARITHMETICAL REASONING
EXAMINATION SECTION
TEST 1

DIRECTIONS: Each question or incomplete statement is followed by several suggested answers or completions. Select the one that BEST answers the question or completes the statement. *PRINT THE LETTER OF THE CORRECT ANSWER IN THE SPACE AT THE RIGHT.*

1. On January 1, a family was receiving supplementary monthly public assistance of $280 for food, $240 for rent, and $140 for other necessities. In the spring, their rent rose by 10%, and their rent allotment was adjusted accordingly. In the summer, due to the death of a family member, their allotments for food and other necessities were reduced by 1/7.
Their monthly allowance check in the fall should be
   A. $623   B. $644   C. $664   D. $684

2. Twice a month, a certain family receives a $340 general allowance for rent, food, and clothing expense. In addition, the family receives a specific supplementary allotment for utilities of $384 a year, which is added to their semi-monthly check.
If the general allowance alone is reduced by 5%, what will be the TOTAL amount of their next semi-monthly check?
   A. $323   B. $339   C. $340   D. $355

3. If each supervising clerk in a certain unit sees an average of 9 clients in a 7-hour day and there are 15 supervising clerks in the unit, APPROXIMATELY how many clients will be seen in a 35-hour week?
   A. 315   B. 405   C. 675   D. 945

4. In one day, an aide receives 18 inquiries by phone and 27 inquiries in person. What percentage of the inquiries received that day were by phone?
   A. 33%   B. 40%   C. 45%   D. 60%

5. If the weekly paychecks for 5 employees are $258.64, $325.48, $287.50, and $313.12, then the combined weekly income for the 5 employee is
   A. $1,455.68   B. $1,456.08   C. $1,462.68   D. $1,474.08

6. Suppose that there are 17 aides working in an office where many community complaints are received by telephone. In one ten-day period, 4,250 calls were received.
If the same number of calls were received each day and the aides divided the work load equally, about how many calls did each aide respond to daily?
   A. 25   B. 35   C. 75   D. 250

7. Suppose that an assignment was divided among 5 aides.
   If the first aide spent 67 hours on the assignment, the second aide spent 95 hours, the third aide spent 52 hours, the fourth aide spent 78 hours, and the fifth aide spent 103 hours, what was the AVERAGE amount of time spent by each aide on the assignment? _____ hours.
   A. 71   B. 75   C. 79   D. 83

   7.____

8. If there are 240 employees in a center and 1/3 are absent on the day of a bad snowstorm, how many employees were at work in the center on that day?
   A. 80   B. 120   C. 160   D. 200

   8.____

9. Suppose that an aide takes 25 minutes to prepare a letter to a client.
   If the aide is assigned to prepare 9 letters on a certain day, how much time should be set aside for this task? _____ hours.
   A. 3¾   B. 4¼   C. 4¾   D. 5¼

   9.____

10. Suppose that a certain center uses both Form A and Form B in the course of its daily work and that Form A is used 4 times as often as Form B.
    If the total number of both forms used in one week is 750, how many times was Form A used?
    A. 100   B. 200   C. 400   D. 600

    10.____

11. Suppose a center has a budget of $2,185.40 from which 8 desks costing $156.10 apiece must be bought.
    How many additional desks can be ordered from this budget after the 8 desks have been purchased?
    A. 4   B. 6   C. 9   D. 14

    11.____

12. When researching a particular case, a team of 16 aides was asked to check through 234 folders to obtain the necessary information.
    If half the aides worked twice as fast as the other half, and the slow group checked through 12 folders each hour, about how long would it take to complete the assignment? _____ hours.
    A. 4¼   B. 5   C. 6   D. 6½

    12.____

13. The difference in the cost of two typewriters is $56.64.
    If the less expensive typewriter costs $307.22, what is the cost of the other typewriter?
    A. $343.86   B. $344.06   C. $363.86   D. $364.06

    13.____

14. At the start of a year, a family was receiving a public assistance grant of $382 twice a month, on the first and fifteenth of each month. On March 1, their rent allowance was decreased from $150 to $142 a month since they had moved to a smaller apartment. On August 1 their semi-monthly food allowance, which had been $80.40, was raised by 10%.
    In that year, the TOTAL amount of money disbursed to this family was
    A. $4,544.20   B. $6,581.40   C. $9,088.40   D. $9,168.40

    14.____

15. It is discovered that a client has received double public assistance for 2 months by having been enrolled at two service centers of the Department of Social Services. The client should have received $168 twice a month instead of the double amount. He now agrees to repay the money by equal deductions from his public assistance check over a period of 12 months.
What will the amount of his NEXT check be?
    A. $112   B. $140   C. $154   D. $160

16. Suppose a study is being made of the composition of 3,550 families receiving public assistance. Of the first 1,050 families reviewed, 18% had four or more children.
If, in the remaining number of families, the percentage with four or more children is half as high as the percentage in the group already reviewed, then the percentage of families with four or more children in the entire group of families is MOST NEARLY
    A. 12   B. 14   C. 16   D. 17

17. Suppose that food prices have risen 13%, and an increase of the same amount has been granted in the food allotment given to people receiving public assistance.
If a family has been receiving $810 a month, 35% of which is allotted for food, then the TOTAL amount of public assistance this family receives per month will be changed to
    A. $805.42   B. $840.06   C. $846.86   D. $899.42

18. Assume that the food allowance is to be raised 5% in August but will be retroactive for four months to April. .
The retroactive allowance is to be divided into equal sections and added to the public assistance checks for August, September, October, November, and December.
A family which has been receiving $840 monthly, 40% of which was allotted for food, will receive what size check in August?
    A. $853.44   B. $856.80   C. $861.00   D. $870.24

19. A blind client, who receives $210 public assistance twice a month, inherits 14 shares of stock worth $180 each. The client is required to sell the stock and spend his inheritance before receiving more public assistance.
Using his public assistance allowance as a guide, how many months are his new assets expected to last?
    A. 6   B. 7   C. 8   D. 12

20. The Department of Social Services has 16 service centers. These centers may be divided into those which are downtown and those which are uptown. Two of the centers are special service centers and are downtown, while the remainder of the centers are general service centers. There is a total of 7 service centers downtown.
The percentage of the general service centers which are uptown is MOST NEARLY
    A. 56   B. 64   C. 69   D. 79

21. For six months, a family lived in a 4-room apartment where they paid $380 a month. They made an intrasite move to a 4-room apartment where they paid $85 per room a month for six months.
Comparing the two six-month periods, the TOTAL amount of money the family saved by making the intrasite was
  A. $240   B. $290   C. $430   D. $590

21._____

22. To calculate a tenant's usable income, you should make Social Security deductions of 4.4 percent on salary up to a maximum of $9,000 and State Disability deductions of .5 percent on salary up to $3,000.
What does a tenant's combined deduction amount to if his annual salary is $13,400?
  A. $411.00   B. $568.60   C. $619.60   D. $700.00

22._____

23. If the temporary relocation expenses for housing are set at $18 per day for one adult and $10 per day for each additional person in a room, how much money is allowed for a woman and four children temporarily relocated in one room for a period of six days?
  A. $168   B. $348   C. $378   D. $518

23._____

24. According to relocation policy, a family relocating to private housing from federally-aided or certain other sites will be granted a relocation payment. This payment equals the difference between 1/5 of the family's yearly income and the scheduled yearly rent for a standard apartment for their size family.
Suppose a 2-person family whose yearly income is $12,900 has been unable to obtain public housing and so finds a one-bedroom private apartment. The scheduled rent for a one-bedroom apartment appropriate for their occupancy is $240 a month.
What payment will they receive?
  A. $240   B. $288   C. $300   D. $410

24._____

25. A family on a housing relocation site is paying $410 per month for rent. This represents 25% of their gross monthly income.
If the husband earns 4/5 of their total combined monthly income, how much does the wife earn per month?
  A. $328   B. $540   C. $1,280   D. $1,500

25._____

KEY (CORRECT ANSWERS)

1.	A	11.	B
2.	B	12.	D
3.	C	13.	C
4.	B	14.	D
5.	B	15.	B
6.	A	16.	A
7.	C	17.	C
8.	C	18.	D
9.	A	19.	A
10.	D	20.	B

21. A
22. A
23. B
24. C
25. A

SOLUTIONS TO PROBLEMS

1. After spring, the rent allotment should be $(240+24) = $264. After the summer, the reduced allotment for food and other necessities should be $[(280+140) − 1/7(280+140)] = $(420−1/7(420)] = $(420−60) = $360. The monthly check in the fall including rent, food, and other necessities should be $360 + $264 = $624.

2. Amount of general allowance in the family's semi-monthly check = $340. Amount of utilities allotment in the family's semi-monthly check: ($\frac{384}{12}$ × ½) = $16. Amount of general allowance in family' semi-monthly check after a 5% reduction = $340 less 5% of $340 = $(340−17) = $3223. Total amount of the next month's semi-monthly check: Reduced general allowance + utilities allotment = $323 + $16 = $339.

3. During 7 hours, a total of (15)(9) = 135 clients can be seen. Thus, in 35 hours, a total of (135)(5) = 675 clients will be seen.

4. 18(18+27) = .40 = 40%

5. $258.64 + $325.48 + $287.34 + $271.50 + $313.12 = $1,456.08

6. 4250/10 = 425 calls per day. Then, 425/17 = 25

7. (67+95+52+78+103)/5 = 79 hours

8. Number present = (240)(2/3) = 160

9. (25)(9) = 225 min. = 3 hrs. 45 min. = 3 ¾ hours

10. Let x, 1/4x = number of forms A, B, respectively. Then, x + 1/4x = 750. Solving, x = 600

11. $2,185.40 − (8)($156.10) = $936.60. Then, $936.60 ÷ $156.10 = 6 desks

12. Since the slow group did 12 folders each hour, the faster group did 24 folders each hour. Then, 234/(12+24) = 6 ½ hrs.

13. Expensive typewriter costs $307.22 + $56.64 = $363.86

14. For months of January and February, the amount the family receives is $(382×2×2) = $1528
    For months of March through July, the family receives $(764−8) × 5 = $3780
    For months August through December, the family receives $(756+16.08) × 5 = $3860.40
    The total amount of money disbursed to this family is $1528 + $3780 + $3860.40 = $9,168.40

15. The overpayment for 2 months = ($168)(4) = $672. If this is paid back over 12 months, each month's amount is reduced by $672/12 = $56. Then, each check (semi-monthly) is reduced by $28. His next check will be $168 − $28 = $140

7 (#1)

16. (1050)(.18) + (2500)(.09) = 414. Then, 414/3550 = 12%

17. ($810)(.35) = $283.50 originally allotted for food. The new food allotment = ($283.50)(1.13) = $320.355. The total assistance now = $810 – $283.50 + $320.355 = $846.855 or $846.86

18. ($840)(.40) = $336 per month for food. The new food allowance = ($336)(1.05) = $352.80 per month. The difference of $16.80 is retroactive to April, which means ($16.80)(9) = $151.20 additional money for August through December. Each check for these 5 months will be increased by $15.20/5 = 30.24. Thus, the check in August = $840 + 30.24 = $840 + 30.24 = $870.24

19. ($180)(14) = $2520. Then, $2520/$420 = 6 months

20. 5 general are downtown; 9 of 14 general are uptown; 9/14 ≈ 64%

21. ($85)(4) = $340 per month. Savings per month = $380 - $340 = $40 For six months, the savings = $240

22. ($9000(.044) + ($3000)(.005) = $411 total deductions

23. ($18+$40)(6) = $348 relocation expenses

24. ($240)(12) – (1/5)($12,900) = $300 relocation payment

25. $410 ÷ .25 = $1640. The wife earns (1640)(1/5) = $328 each month

TEST 2

DIRECTIONS: Each question or incomplete statement is followed by several suggested answers or completions. Select the one that BEST answers the question or completes the statement. *PRINT THE LETTER OF THE CORRECT ANSWER IN THE SPACE AT THE RIGHT.*

1. A project tenant who owns and drives a taxicab for living, reports for a three-month period an income of $6,250 after operating expenses of $1,300 have been considered. In addition, his tips are valued at 12% of his income before operating expenses.
   An estimate of his yearly income is MOST NEARLY
   A. $22,000 B. $23,000 C. $28,000
   D. $28,500 E. $29,000

   1.____

2. The maximum annual subsidy which can be paid by the State toward the operation of any low-rent housing project is the sum of the annual interest on the total original loan or building the project and 1% of the portion of the loan actually spent.
   If the original loan for a project was $8,000,000 at 1¾% interest, but only $7,500,000 was actually spent, then the MAXIMUM annual subsidy is
   A. $140,000 B. $145,000 C. $215,000
   D. $220,000 E. $271,250

   2.____

3. In 2020, the cost of repairs and maintenance at a certain housing project was $5,589 more than in 2019, representing an increase of 4.6%. A further increase at the same rate was anticipated for 2021.
   The cost of repairs and maintenance in 2021 was MOST NEARLY
   A. $127,100
   B. $132,700
   C. $132,900
   D. $133,000
   E. an amount which cannot be determined from the given data

   3.____

4. Each day a delivery truck used by the Housing Authority travels 25 miles from a project to a storehouse and 25 miles on the return trip. It travels at the rate of 30 miles per hour going to the storehouse and at the rate of 20 miles per hour returning.
   The average rate, in miles per hour, for the roundtrip is MOST NEARLY
   A. 24
   B. 25
   C. 26
   D. the square root of 600
   E. an amount which cannot be determined from the given data

   4.____

5. A report on the first 6,000 applications for apartments in a certain project containing 1,400 apartments indicated that those who were ineligible fell into four categories: 2,800 ineligible for reason A, 600 ineligible for reason B, 1,200 ineligible for reason C, and 400 ineligible for reason D.

   5.____

138

2 (#2)

If the same proportions continue for the remaining 21,500 applications, then the percentage of eligible applicants who can be given apartments in the project is MOST NEARLY
 A. 25 B. 30 C. 33 D. 40 E. 60

6. The number of applications for apartments in low-rent housing projects was 40,000 in 2019. The number of applications increased 5% in 2020, and increased again in 2021 by 6% over the 2,000 total.
The percentage by which the 2021 figures exceed the 2019 figures is
 A. 5.3 B. 6.0 C. 11.0 D. 11.3 E. 30.0

6.____

7. A rectangular lot, 75 feet by 11.0 feet, was purchased as part of a project site for $28,500.
The price per square foot of this lot is MOST NEARLY
 A. $2.85 B. $3.45 C. $3.95 D. $30.00 E. $30.95

7.____

8. It has been estimated that 125 kilowatt-hours of electricity are used each month in one average Housing Authority apartment at a cost of 14.8 cents per kilowatt-hour.
On this basis, the total cost of the electricity used in one year in a project containing 1,400 apartments is MOST NEARLY
 A. $20,000 B. $25,000 C. $200,000
 D. $250,000 E. $2,000,000

8.____

9. The walls and ceilings of 20 rooms are to be painted with the same kind of paint, each room being 15 feet long, 12 feet wide, and 10 feet high. Each room contains two windows, each 3 feet by 6 feet, and a door 3 feet by 8 feet, which are not to be painted. One gallon of paint covers 400 square feet of surface.
The number of gallons of paint needed is MOST NEARLY
 A. 33 B. 34 C. 35 D. 36 E. 75

9.____

10. A group of buildings is valued at $11,500,000. Assume that the cos of fire insurance for these buildings is 5.3 cents per $100 of valuation per year.
The cost of fire insurance for one year is MOST NEARLY
 A. $600 B. $6,000 C. $20,000
 D. $60,000 E. $2,000,000

10.____

11. Of the 15 employees in a certain unit, one-third earn $27,600 per year, three earn $32,600, one earns $46,400, and the rest earn $33,800.
The average salary of the employees of this unit is MOST NEARLY
 A. $31,000 B. $32,000 C. $33,000 D. $34,000 E. $35,000

11.____

12. Four pieces, each 2'8½" long, are cut from a piece of pipe 16½' long.
The length of the remaining piece of pipe is
 A. 6'8½" B. 6'10" C. 6'10⅜" D. 6'11⅛" E. 9'9½"

12.____

13. A tenant ears E dollars a month, spends S dollars a week, and saves the rest. The tenant's yearly savings can be expressed by
    A. 12(E-4S) B. 12E – 52S C. 12(E-S)
    D. 52(E-4S) E. E - S

14. A unit of fifteen Housing Assistants has been assigned the job of interviewing applicants. Each interview takes 35 minutes, and an additional 10 minutes is needed for making entries and notes. The last interview each day is always scheduled so that it can be completed that day.
    The number of applicants who can be interviewed in a week, consisting of five 7-hour days, is MOST NEARLY
    A. 375 B. 525 C. 675 D. 700 E. 725

15. A review of the 14,000 applications for apartments in a certain project containing 1,200 apartments indicated that 4,800 applicants were eligible and 6,400 were ineligible. No decision could be reached on the remaining applications because certain necessary information was omitted by the applicants, but it was assumed that the proportion of eligible and ineligible applicants would remain the same as in those already decided.
    On the basis of these figures, the percentage of eligible applicants who can be given apartments in the project is
    A. under 17% B. 17% C. 20%
    D. 25% E. 33 1/3%

16. An oil burner in a housing development burns 76 gallons of fuel oil per hour. At 9 A.M. on a very cold day, the superintendent asks the Housing Manager to put in an emergency order for more fuel oil. At that time, he reports that he has on hand 266 gallons. At noon, he again comes to the manager, notifying him that no oil has been delivered.
    The MAXIMUM amount of time that he can continue to furnish heat without receiving more oil is
    A. no more time B. ½ hour C. 1 hour
    D. 1½ hours E. 2 hours

17. As a result of reports received by the Housing Authority concerning the reputed ineligibility of 756 tenants because of above-standard incomes, an intensive check of their employers has been ordered. Four housing assistants have been assigned to this task. At the end of 6 days at 7 hours each, they have checked on 336 tenants. In order to speed up the investigation, two more housing assistants are assigned to this point.
    If they worked at the same rate, the number of additional 7-hour days it would take to complete the job is MOST NEARLY
    A. 1 B. 3 C. 5 D. 7 E. 9

4 (#2)

18. A municipal aide on a special trip is returning to his office from a point 17½ miles away, and makes the return trip to his office at an average speed of 25 miles an hour, except for a 15-minute stopover at one point to get a flat tire fixed. The time it should take him to reach his office is MOST NEARLY _____ minutes.
    A. 12   B. 22   C. 36   D. 42   E. 57

18._____

19. A district office has an assigned staff of 320 employees. Of this number, 25% are not available for duty due to illness, vacations, and other reasons. Of those who are available for duty, 1/8 are assigned to auditing and special projects, and the rest to handling the workload.
    The ACTUAL number of employees available for handling the workload is
    A. 350   B. 310   C. 270   D. 210   E. 180

19._____

20. Two dozen shuttlecocks and four badminton rackets are to be purchased for a playground. The shuttlecocks are priced at $3.60 each, and the rackets at $27.50 each. The playground receives a discount of 30% from these prices.
    The TOTAL cost of this equipment is
    A. $72.90   B. $114.30   C. $137.48   D. $186.00   E. $220.70

20._____

21. On January 1, a family was receiving public assistance allowance of $185 for food, $53 for clothing, $17.50 for utilities, and $22 for personal needs, all semi-monthly, and a monthly allowance of $550 for rent. On May 1, the rent allowance was increased by 12% but all other allowances remained the same for the rest of the year.
    The TOTAL amount of money granted this family during the year was
    A. $10,528   B. $13,262   C. $13,788
    D. $21,056   E. $27,676

21._____

22. It has been decided to make changes in food allotments to clients receiving public assistance to conform to changes in food costs. Of the food allowance, 30% is intended for meat, 30% for fruits and vegetables, 25% for groceries, and 15% for dairy products. Assume that meat prices have gone up 5%, and dairy prices have remained the same.
    For a family that has been receiving $400 per month for food, the new monthly food allowance will be
    A. $333   B. $375   C. $393   D. $403.50   E. $420

22._____

23. On January 1, a family was receiving a public assistance allowance of $195 for food, $63 for clothing, $27.50 for utilities, and $32 for personal needs, all semi-monthly, and a monthly allowance of $510 for rent. On June 1, the rent allowance was increased by 12%, but all other allowances remained the same for the rest of the year.
    The TOTAL amount of money granted this family during the year was
    A. $13,843.40   B. $14,107.20   C. $14,168.40
    D. $14,474.40   E. $16,886.80

23._____

5 (#2)

24. A member of a family receiving public assistance amounting to $600 monthly has obtained a part-time job, for which he is paid $40 a day. He is employed 3 days a week. His carfare costs $3.00 per day and his lunches $2.00 per day. Assume that there are $4\frac{1}{3}$ weeks per month. The Department of Welfare requires that net earnings be deducted from relief allowances.
The family's semi-monthly public assistance allowances should be reduced to
A. $40.00   B. $72.50   C. $96.25   D. $123.75   E. $145.00

24._____

25. A couple living in a furnished room has been receiving a public assistance grant of $375 semi-monthly and has been paying a weekly rent of $75. The landlord has been granted a 12% increase in rent. Assume that a month consists of $4\frac{1}{3}$ weeks.
The amount of the new semi-monthly grant, including this rent increase, that the couple will receive will be MOST NEARLY
A. $394.50   B. $397   C. $409   D. $514   E. $557

25._____

KEY (CORRECT ANSWERS)

1.	D		11.	B
2.	C		12.	A
3.	C		13.	B
4.	A		14.	C
5.	B		15.	C
6.	D		16.	B
7.	B		17.	C
8.	D		18.	E
9.	A		19.	D
10.	B		20.	C

21. C
22. C
23. C
24. B
25. A

SOLUTIONS TO PROBLEMS

1. For 3 months, income = $6,250 + (.12)($7550) = $7156. Then, annual income = ($7154)(4) = $28,624, closest to $28,500.

2. Maximum annual subsidy = ($8,000,000)(.0175) + (.01)($7,500,000) = $215,000

3. Cost in 2019 = $5589/.046 = $121,500. The cost in 2020 = $121,500 + $5589 = $127,089. This means the cost in 2021 = ($127,089)(1.046) = $132,900

4. Average rate = total distance/total time = (25+25) ÷ (25/30 + 25/20) = 24 mph

5. Out of 600, number of eligible = 6000 – 2800 – 600 – 1200 – 400 = 1000. Thus, for 27,500 applications, (1/6)(27,500) = 4583 would be eligible. Finally, 1400 ÷ 4583 ≈ 30%

6. Number of applications in 2020 = (40,000)(1.05) = 42,000. Number of applications in 2021 = (42,000)(1.06) = 44,520. Then, (44,520–40,000) ÷ 40,000 = 11.3%

7. $28,500 ÷ [(75×110)] = $3.45 per sq. ft.

8. Total cost = (125)(.148)(12)(1400) = $310,800; closest to choice D of $250,000

9. Painted area of each room = (2)(15)(10) + (2)(12)(10) + (15)(12) − (2)(3)(6) − (3)(8) = 660 sq. ft. So, (20)(660) = 13,200 sq. ft. to be painted in all rooms. Finally, 13,200/400 = 33 gallons of paint needed

10. Insurance cost = (.053)($11,500,000)/$100 = $6095, closest to $6000

11. [(5)($27,600) + (3)($32,600) + (1)($46,400) + (6)($33,800)]/15 = $32,233 closest to $32,000

12. 16½ - (4)(2'5³/₈") = 16'6" − 8'21½" = 16'6" − 9'9½" = 6'8½"

13. Annual savings = 12E − 52S

14. 7 ÷ ¾ = 9.$\overline{3}$, which means each interviewer can interview a maximum of 9 applicants each day. Then, (5)(9)(15) = 675 applicants

15. 4800/(4800+6400) = 3/7 eligible. On that assumption, there would be (3/7)(14,000) = 6000 eligible applicants. Then, 1200/6000 = 20%

16. 266 − (3)(76) = 38 gallons of oil left. Then, 38/76 = ½ hour

17. (6)(7)(4) = 168 hours to check on 336 tenants. This means 2 tenants require 1 man-hour. Now, (6)(7)(x days) = man-hours would be needed to check the remaining 420 tenants. This requires 210 man-hours. So, (6)(7)(x) = 210. Solving, x = 5

18. $\frac{17.5}{25}$ = .7 hr. = 42 min. Total time = 42 + 15 = 57 minutes.

7 (#2)

19. Number available = 320[1-.25(1/8)(.75) = 210

20. Total cost = (.70)[(24)($3.60)+(4)(27.50)] = $137.48

21. From January through April, amount = (8)($185+$53+$17.50+$22) + (4)($550) = $4420. From May through December, amount = (16)($185+$53+17.50+$22) + (8)($550)(1.12) = $9368. Total annual amount = $4420 + $9368 = $13,788

22. Meat allowance = ($400)(.30)(1.10) = $132; fruit and vegetable allowance = ($400)(.30)(.80) = $96; grocery allowance = ($400)(.25)(1.05) = $105; dairy allowance = ($400)(.15) = $60. New monthly allowance = $132 + $96 + $105 + $.60 = $393

23. From January through May, amount = (10)($195+$63+$27.50+$32) + (5)($510) = $5725. From June through December, amount = (14)($195+$63+$27.50+$32) + (7)($510)(1.12) = $8443.40. Total annual amount = $5725 + $8443.40 = $14,168.40

24. Monthly assistance should be reduced to $600 − [(40)(3)($4^{1}/_{3}$) − ($5)(3)($4^{1}/_{3}$)] = $145. So, the semi-monthly amount is now $145/2 = $72.50

25. ($75)($4^{1}/_{3}$)/2 = original semi-monthly rent.
New semi-monthly rent = (162.50)(1.12) = $182. Since this represents an increase of $19.50, the new semi-monthly grant will be increased to $375 + $19.50 = $394.50

INTERPRETING STATISTICAL DATA
GRAPHS, CHARTS AND TABLES

EXAMINATION SECTION
TEST 1

DIRECTIONS: Each question or incomplete statement is followed by several suggested answers or completions. Select the one that BEST answers the question or completes the statement. *PRINT THE LETTER OF THE CORRECT ANSWER IN THE SPACE AT THE RIGHT.*

Questions 1-6.

DIRECTIONS: Questions 1 through 6 deal with social service allowances of various kinds. Assuming that in the Department of Social Services the allowance schedules shown below are among those included in estimating the needs of relief recipients, use the figures given to determine your answers. All figures are quoted on a monthly basis.

Item	Allowance
Rent	As paid by client
Utilities	$9.60 per person
Person Incidentals	$5.60 per person

	Adult	Child 13-18	Child under 13
Food	$288.00	$280.00	$240.00
Clothing	$72.00	$67.20	$63.20

1. The Anderson family, consisting of father, mother, and four children aged 4, 10, 15, and 17, is eligible for home relief. The rent is $640 a month. Relief granted on the basis of the above items is given semi-monthly. According to the schedule shown, the PROPER semi-monthly grant for this family would be

   A. $860.80   B. $1141.60   C. $1373.60   D. $2507.20

   1._____

2. Assuming that all the expenditures except rent were reimbursable under the State Welfare Law to the same extent that reimbursements for home relief are now being made to the city, the annual cost to the city for all the items included in the public assistance budget of the Anderson family would be APPROXIMATELY

   A. $6720   B. $12,800   C. $19,200   D. $22,400

   2._____

3. Mrs. Peet is 67 years old and applies for old age assistance. She lives with her widowed niece, who has a family of three children. The rent of the apartment is $448 a month. The niece has agreed to pay for the utilities of the whole group and also to give Mrs. Peet some money for personal incidentals, provided that Mrs. Peet can pay one-fifth of the rent. On medical advice, a special diet allowance of $61.76 a month is authorized for Mrs.Peet in addition to the regular food allowance.
   The PROPER monthly grant for Mrs. Peet would be

   A. $399.04   B. $448.60   C. $511.36   D. $805.20

   3._____

145

4. Mrs. Scalise applies for relief for herself and her two children, aged two and four. Her rent costs $420 a month. She is separated from her husband, who contributes $144 a week by court order. It has also been verified that Mrs. Scalise earns $89.60 a week doing piecework at home. Assuming that for budget computation purposes the Department of Social Services considers 4.3 weeks as equivalent to one month, the monthly grant in this case would be

   A. $430.48   B. $527.52   C. $750.40   D. $809.76

5. A 36-year-old sightless widower applies for aid to the blind. His rent and utilities are met by relatives with whom he lives. In aid to blind cases, $73.60 per month is allowed for expenses incident to blindness as a substitute for the personal incidentals item in the schedule above.
   Under these circumstances, the PROPER monthly grant would be computed at

   A. $274.00   B. $429.60   C. $517.20   D. $846.00

6. John Burke is 52 years old and needs supplementary home relief. He pays $296 a month for his room, and he earns $336 a month doing odd jobs.
   Basing your computations on these facts and on the schedule above, you can determine that the PROPER semi-monthly grant for Mr. Burke would be

   A. $406.80   B. $295.68   C. $169.60   D. $130.40

KEY (CORRECT ANSWERS)

1. C
2. B
3. C
4. B
5. B
6. C

TEST 2

Questions 1-6.

DIRECTIONS: Questions 1 through 6 are to be answered SOLELY on the basis of the following table, which shows the Total Monthly Rent Roll and the Number of Tenants at each of six housing projects in City X.

Project	Total Monthly Rent Roll	Number of Tenants
Bryant	$604,840	1,796
Dansforth	517,784	1,482
Glendale	784,548	2,220
Lowell	527,592	1,534
Main Street	709,860	2,310
Swift Towers	367,800	1,240

1. The average monthly rent per tenant at the Swift Towers Project is MOST NEARLY

   A. $280.80 B. $288.04 C. $296.60 D. $300.24

2. Suppose that at the end of the first week of the month, the following amounts of current rent have been collected at four of the projects:
   Bryant $573,680
   Glendale $748,872
   Lowell $491,796
   Swift Towers $331,856
   At which project did the GREATEST amount of money still have to be paid toward the Total Monthly Rent Roll?

   A. Bryant B. Glendale C. Lowell D. Swift Towers

3. The average monthly rental per tenant at these six projects is MOST NEARLY

   A. $323.84 B. $326.96 C. $331.92 D. $333.64

4. If current rent was collected at the Dansforth Project during the first week of the month from 1,435 tenants whose average rent is $348.00 per month, then the percentage of the Total Monthly Rent Roll collected during this week is MOST NEARLY

   A. 95.54% B. 96.45% C. 96.83% D. 97.11%

5. Assume that during the first four business days of the month, the following amounts of current rent had been paid by cash or check at the Main Street Project:

	Paid in Cash	Paid by Check
1st Day	$24,776	$103,368
2nd Day	$28,920	$ 75,452
3rd Day	$23,852	$ 86,524
4th Day	$35,664	$110,972

147

The amount of the Total Monthly Rent Roll which still remained to be collected after these four days was MOST NEARLY

    A. $220,332   B. $222,440   C. $224,444   D. $227,672

6. If it is expected that 2% of the tenants will fail to pay their current rent during the first week of the month at the Glendale and Main Street Projects, and 2.5% of the tenants at the Bryant and Lowell Projects will similarly fail to pay their rent during the first week of the month, at which project will the LARGEST number of tenants still have to pay rent at the end of the first week?

    A. Bryant   B. Glendale   C. Lowell   D. Main Street

KEY (CORRECT ANSWERS)

1. C
2. D
3. C
4. B
5. A
6. D

TEST 3

Questions 1-5.

DIRECTIONS: Questions 1 through 5 are to be answered SOLELY on the basis of the following table of rent collections. Project X has 1,920 tenants with a total monthly rent roll of $460,216. Cash collections of current rents for the FIRST WEEK of the month were as follows:

	Cash Collections	Number of Tenants
Monday	$ 44,160	198
Tuesday	$ 68,412	287
Wednesday	$112,740	455
Thursday	$ 86,520	354
Friday	$139,088	589

1. The percentage increase in Tuesday's collections over Monday's collections was MOST NEARLY

    A. 35.4%   B. 44.9%   C. 54.9%   D. 63.1%

2. The percentage of the total monthly rent roll that was collected on the largest collection day was MOST NEARLY

    A. 30.2%   B. 30.7%   C. 30.8%   D. 31.3%

3. The percentage of tenants who did not pay their rent in the first week of the month was MOST NEARLY

    A. 1.9%   B. 2%   C. 19.3%   D. 98.1%

4. The average monthly rental per apartment at Project X is MOST NEARLY

    A. $239.48   B. $239.68   C. $241.76   D. $244.40

5. If the cash was collected daily by the same three tellers and if at the end of the week each teller had collected approximately the same amount, the average daily collection for each teller was MOST NEARLY

    A. $30,061.32   B. $30,681.08
    C. $90,184.00   D. $150,306.68

KEY (CORRECT ANSWERS)

1. C
2. A
3. A
4. B
5. A

TEST 4

Questions 1-5.

DIRECTIONS: Questions 1 through 5 are to be answered SOLELY on the basis of the following table.

Category of Assistance	City A	City B	City C	City D	City E
Home Relief	10,476	13,694	8,403	5,572	4,809
Veteran Assistance	2,362	1,719	1,451	1,127	843
Old Age Assistance	12,698	13,428	9,762	6,891	5,619
Aid to the Blind	987	642	328	472	216
Aid to Dependent Children	62,198	43,271	37,298	10,987	2,634
Aid to the Disabled	9,654	6,842	3.476	5,020	1,983
TOTAL	98,375	79,596	60,718	29,169	16,104

1. The number of cases receiving Old Age Assistance is GREATER than the total number receiving Home Relief and Veteran Assistance combined in City

   A. A B. C C. D D. E

2. If the cities were ranked in accordance with the number of cases in the category of Aid to the Blind (highest number to rank first), the city which would follow City B would be

   A. A B. C C. D D. E

3. Of all the cases receiving Veteran Assistance, the percentage of those receiving Veteran Assistance who live in City A is MOST NEARLY

   A. 15% B. 20% C. 25% D. 30%

4. The number of cities in which the number of Old Age Assistance cases is more than twice the number of Aid to the Disabled cases is

   A. 1 B. 2 C. 3 D. 4

5. The number of categories of assistance in which the number of cases in City A is more than 10% higher than the number of cases in City B is

   A. 2 B. 3 C. 4 D. 5

KEY (CORRECT ANSWERS)

1. C
2. C
3. D
4. B
5. C

TEST 5

Questions 1-5.

DIRECTIONS: Questions 1 through 5 are to be answered SOLELY on the basis of the following table.

NUMBER OF PUBLICLY AND PRIVATELY BUILT DWELLING UNITS IN REGION A						
	UNITS IN PUBLIC HOUSING			UNITS IN PRIVATE HOUSING		
	Subsidized	Unsubsidized			Apartment 1 to 3 Family	
Year	Projects	Projects	Total	Houses	Homes	Total
2009	13,960	4,390	18,350	890	7,600	8,490
2010	15,000	5,910	20,910	920	7,720	8,640
2011	16,790	7,500	24,290	980	7,940	8,920
2012	19,420	8,710	28,130	1,050	8,090	9,140
2013	21,110	9,870	30,980	1,240	8,300	9,540
2014	22,910	10,460	33,370	1,570	8,350	9,920
2015	24,870	12,980	37,850	2,010	9,760	11,770
2016	27,620	14,270	41,890	2,970	10,140	13,110
2017	29,480	15,120	44,600	4,020	12,340	16,360
2018	30,580	16,380	46,960	5,870	15,400	21,270
TOTALS	?	105,590	327,330	21,520	95,640	117,160

1. For the ten-year period in the table, the yearly average number of public housing units built exceeded the yearly number of private housing units built by MOST NEARLY

   A. 12,500 B. 15,000 C. 20,000 D. 21,000

2. Over the entire ten-year period in the above table, the ratio of the total number of units built in 1 to 3 family homes to the total number of units built in all other types in the table combined was MOST NEARLY

   A. 1:2 B. 1:3 C. 1:4 D. 2:5

3. The number of years during which the number of units built in all private housing exceeded the number built in unsubsidized projects was

   A. 2 B. 4 C. 6 D. 8

4. In 2015, in the region covered by the table, the average monthly rent was $428 in privately constructed apartment houses and $328 in unsubsidized public housing projects. The total monthly rent for the units built in 2015 in these two categories was MOST NEARLY

   A. $4,800,000
   B. $5,500,000
   C. $8,322,800
   D. $9,000,000

5. The year during which there was the GREATEST increase from the previous year in the number of units built in one-to-three family homes was 5.____

   A. 2010   B. 2012   C. 2016   D. 2018

KEY (CORRECT ANSWERS)

1. D
2. C
3. C
4. A
5. D

TEST 6

Questions 1-5.

DIRECTIONS: Questions 1 through 5 are to be answered SOLELY on the basis of the data given in the table below.

DWELLING UNITS BUILT IN THE CITY AND THE UNITED STATES
1995-2010

	NUMBER BUILT			INDEX (1931 = 100)	
Year	City	United States	City As A % of U.S.	City	United States
1995	16,892	221,000	7.6	32.9	49.2
1996	33,309	319,000	10.4	64.9	71.0
1997	38,354	336,000	11.4	74.7	74.8
1998	64,593	406,000	15.9	125.8	90.4
1999	42,089	515,000	8.2	81.9	114.7
2000	36,964	603,000	6.1	72.0	134.3
2001	23,154	706,000	3.3	45.1	147.2
2002	6,005	356,000	1.7	11.7	79.3
2003	33	191,000	0.02	0.06	42.5
2004	150	142,000	0.1	0.3	31.6
2005	1,832	209,000	0.9	3.6	46.5
2006	28,952	670,000	4.3	56.4	149.2
2007	18,090	849,000	2.1	35.2	189.1
2008	25,809	932,000	2.8	50.3	207.6
2009	44,168	1,025,000	4.3	86.0	228.3
2010	39,408	1,396,000	2.8	76.7	310.0

1. The number of years during which there was a decrease from the previous year of at least 10% in the number of dwelling units built in the city is

   A. 3   B. 5   C. 6   D. 7

2. The number of years during which the index of dwelling units built in the whole country was more than three times as large as the city index is

   A. 6   B. 8   C. 10   D. 11

3. The year in which there was the GREATEST percentage increase over the previous year in the number of dwellings built, both in the city and in the whole country, is

   A. 1998   B. 2004   C. 2005   D. 2006

4. Considering only the first ten years of the table, the number of years in which the index of dwelling units built was HIGHER for the whole country than for the city is

   A. 1   B. 8   C. 9   D. 10

154

5. Assume that in 2011 the number of dwelling units built in the city represented a percentage of the whole country equal to twice the 2010 percentage.
If the number of dwelling units built in the city was 26,500, then the number built in the entire country was MOST NEARLY

   A. 475,000   B. 675,000   C. 900,000   D. 1,000,000

5._____

KEY (CORRECT ANSWERS)

1. D
2. B
3. D
4. C
5. A

TEST 7

Questions 1-5.

DIRECTIONS: Questions 1 through 5 are to be answered SOLELY on the basis of the following three charts concerning referrals made by the Department of Welfare of the City of Millville.

TABLE 1
REFERRALS MADE FOR SPECIALIZED HELP

	Number of Referrals For			
Year	Psychiatric Help	Alcoholism	Vocational Rehabilitation	Homemaking Service
2013	110	60	180	20
2014	120	36	205	36
2015	80	25	275	40
2016	90	16	250	40
2017	100	5	230	38

TABLE 2
RESULTS OF REFERRALS FOR VOCATIONAL REHABILITATION

Year	Total Referrals	Appeared For Initial Interviews	Kept Appointments, Cooperative	Treatment Successful	Off Welfare As Result of Treatment
2013	180	120	40	30	25
2014	205	180	120	80	60
2015	275	220	160	120	100
2016	250	215	160	130	105
2017	230	220	170	128	90

TABLE 3

AVERAGE PERCENTAGE OF *BUDGET FOR SPECIALIZED HELP* EXPENDED ON EACH CATEGORY (FOR THE FIVE YEAR PERIOD 2013-2017)

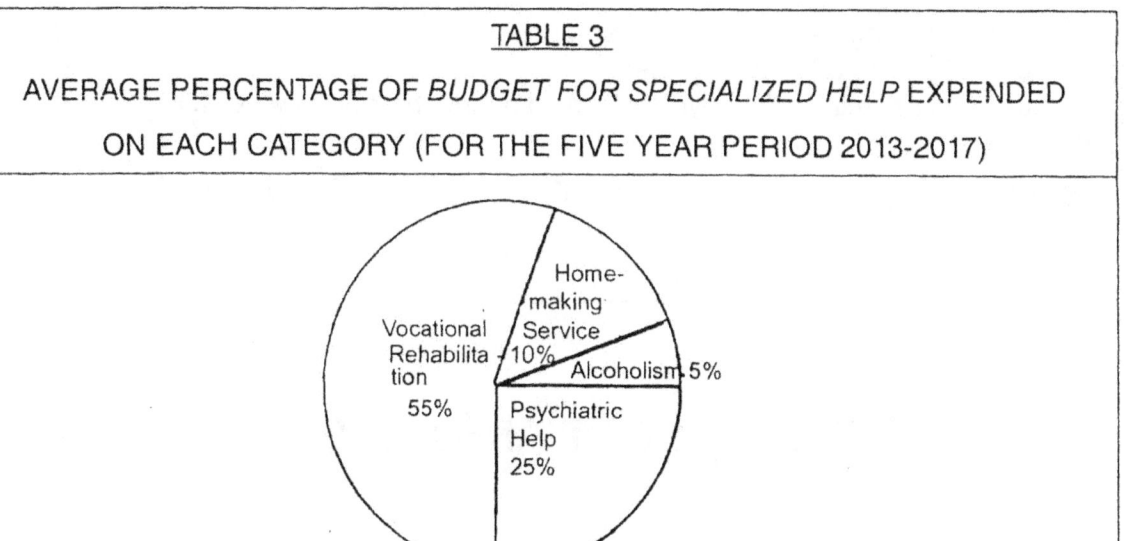

1. Of the following, the two years when an equal percentage of clients who were cooperative when referred for vocational rehabilitation were successfully treated were

   A. 2013 and 2014
   B. 2013 and 2015
   C. 2014 and 2016
   D. 2015 and 2016

2. If in 2016 the number of referrals had been increased for alcoholism by 10, for vocational rehabilitation by 40, and for homemaking services by 5, then the total number of referrals for specialized help that year would have increased by MOST NEARLY

   A. 1.5%   B. 7%   C. 14%   D. 30%

3. Although there are actually no errors in the charts given above, suppose that one of the following figures was recorded incorrectly and constituted the one and only error in the charts.
   By carefully inspecting the charts, one could ALWAYS tell that there was an error, if the error was made in the figure for the

   A. average percentage utilization for psychiatric help of the *Budget for Specialized Help* from 2013 through 2017
   B. number of referrals for alcoholism in 2017
   C. number of referrals for vocational rehabilitation who were removed from welfare as a result of treatment in 2015
   D. number referred for vocational rehabilitation in 2016 who appeared for initial interview

4. In 2015, the budget for specialized help was $200,000, and the amount expended for vocational rehabilitation was $8,000 more than the amount represented by the average percentage expended for vocational rehabilitation for the period 2013 through 2017. The amount expended for vocational rehabilitation in 2015 was MOST NEARLY

   A. $4,400   B. $19,000   C. $44,000   D. $118,000

5. Assume that the average size of the budget for specialized help for the five-year period 2013 through 2017 was $360,000 per year.
The average cost per referral for psychiatric help during this period was MOST NEARLY

   A. $180
   B. $360
   C. $720
   D. $900

KEY (CORRECT ANSWERS)

1. B
2. C
3. D
4. D
5. D

CHILD SUPPORT SERVICES – OVERVIEW

Every child is entitled to financial and emotional support from both parents. This is true even if the child's parents do not live together and were never married. Child support is the amount of money the court decides the non-custodial parent owes to the person caring for their child (the custodial parent). In many states, parents are responsible for supporting their child until the child is 21 years old.

The child support enforcement agency helps people establish paternity, establish child support orders, obtain medical support coverage for their children, collect child support payments, and take actions against people who should pay child support and are not paying. Every state has child support agencies and many foreign countries do too. All of the states and most foreign countries help each other collect child support.

Any parent, guardian, or caretaker of a child for whom child support is needed is eligible to apply for and receive child support services. Also, if a person applies for temporary or safety net assistance for themselves, or on behalf of a child with whom they reside, they are automatically sent to the child support agency for child support services. If seeking child support may result in physical or emotional harm to the custodial parent or their child, the custodial parent will be referred to a domestic violence liaison, and may not be required to cooperate with the child support agency.

ESTABLISHING PATERNITY

The information above and that follows below will help you address your client's questions and concerns regarding child support and the role of the father and the courts in child support services:

What is child support? What is the child support enforcement agency?
Who can apply for child support services?
Am I the legal father of my child?
Why should I legally acknowledge paternity?
What if I am not sure or do not think the child is mine?
If I am the father, when do I have to go to court? What happens at court?
How much will I have to pay?
What if I don't go to the court hearing? What happens at the hearing?
What if I can't pay my child support? Will the amount I owe change?
What if I move?
What if I do not pay what I am supposed to?

Even though the child's mother (and father) know who the father of the child is, unless they are married, he is not the legal father of the child. So unless he does certain things, he will not be the legal father of the child. The easiest way to become the legal father of the child is for he and the mother of the child to fill out or complete a voluntary Acknowledgment of Paternity. This form can be completed any time after the child is born, at a hospital, clinic, child support agency office, family court, or birth registrar's office. If the mother was married at any time during her pregnancy, or at the time of birth, he must go to court to establish paternity. Completing the Acknowledgment of Paternity will also give him legal rights as a parent. It will allow him to have his name on his child's birth certificate, to seek court-ordered visitation and custody, and to have a say in adoption proceedings. By signing the voluntary Acknowledgment of Paternity form, he also takes responsibility for supporting the child until the age required by the state.

The most important reason to legally acknowledge paternity is to show respect for the child. His child will know that he cared enough to become their legal father. Also, the child will be able to have benefits that are available through the father, as their parent, such as health insurance through his employer and money from social security. If he is not sure or does not think he is the father of the child, he should not sign the Acknowledgment of Paternity form. He or the person taking care of the child can start a court action to decide the issue of paternity. If this action is taken, he will have to appear in court. He has the right to hire a lawyer for this action, if he is unable to afford a lawyer, state laws generally provide that the court may assign him one.

When he appears in court, the court will order him, the mother and the child to submit to certain genetic or DNA tests. Based on the genetic or DNA tests and other evidence, the court will decide whether or not he is legally the father of the child. If he is not the father, the court will dismiss the action brought against him. If he is the father, the court will issue an order of filiation, which says he is the child's father. After the order of filiation is issued, the court will decide how much he will have to pay for child support. If he is the legal parent of a child and does not live with the child, he or the other parent or the person who is taking care of the child can go to court to get a court order for child support. The court order will set the amount he has to pay for child support.

If someone besides the father starts a court action to get him to pay child support, he will find out about it by getting two documents-a petition and a summons. The petition shows that someone has asked a court to make an order against him. The summons tells him that he must come to court for a hearing about this. At court, a hearing will be held to figure out how much he will have to pay for child support. He should bring his latest tax returns, W-2s, paycheck stubs, and everything else he has to show his current income. The judge or hearing examiner will use this information and other information presented by other parties to figure out what he should pay for child support for his child.

Once the father is under a court order for child support, he must notify the child support enforcement agency if he changes his residential and/or mailing address, telephone number, social security number, or driver's license number. Your client's obligation to support his child begins when his child is born. If he does not start paying support when the child is born, or does not pay what he owes for pregnancy or birth expenses, the amount he should have paid starts to add up. The child support enforcement agency keeps track of the money he owes. Amounts he owes that he has not paid are called arrears. If he has arrears, the child support enforcement agency will take steps to collect that money. These steps can include: taking tax refunds, lottery winnings, and bank accounts; suspending his driver's license; and notifying credit reporting agencies about his debt. If he does not pay support, he can also be sentenced to time in jail.

THE CHILD SUPPORT ENFORCEMENT PROGRAM

The child support enforcement program was established by Congress in 1975 as Title IV-D of the Social Security Act, and requires all States to enact laws and to implement procedures for the establishment of paternity, and the establishment, enforcement, and collection of child support. As required by Title IV-D, all states must have a child support enforcement program.

Local administration of the program is carried out by local social services districts through their child support enforcement units (CSEU). State Division of Child Support Enforcement (DCSE) ensures that all federal and State requirements are being completed by the local district child support enforcement units by performing the following functions:
* Monitoring and assessing performance levels
* Providing technical assistance and program support
* Operating a statewide computer system
* Providing centralized services
* Issuing regulations, policies, and procedures
* Providing child support training
* Administering program funding

Within each of the local social services districts, the child support enforcement units are responsible for providing the child support enforcement services. Among these services are:

* Creating computerized case files
* Initiating location searches
* Interviewing recipients of services and non-custodial parents
* Preparing and filing paternity and support petitions, affidavits, and orders
* Providing legal services
* Preparing and filing acknowledgments of paternity
* Monitoring cases for support compliance
* Administering support collections
* Providing payment information
* Issuing administrative enforcement notices
* Referring cases to the New York State Department of Taxation and Finance
* Issuing orders for DNA or genetic marker testing in contested paternity cases
* Issuing subpoenas for information
* Accessing information from government agencies
* Accessing employment and financial records

Once an individual applies for child support services, the child support program, free of charge, provides the following services. The provision of these services is a joint effort between the State Division of Child Support Enforcement and each of the local district Child Support Enforcement Units:

Location Investigation: If the custodial parent does not know where the non-custodial parent or putative (alleged) father lives, child support will attempt to locate them. Child support will attempt to locate them through inquiries at the last known address and place of employment, and through other local efforts. Child support also uses federal, State, and local resources to help locate the non-custodial parent or putative (alleged) father.

Paternity Establishment: For children born to unmarried parents, unless paternity is established, there is no legal relationship between the father and the child. This legal relationship can be established either by completing a voluntary Acknowledgment of Paternity form or by filing a paternity petition in court. Child support staff can assist unmarried parents complete and file a voluntary Acknowledge of Paternity form, or, if there is any doubt regarding the identity of the father, child support staff can assist either parent file a paternity petition to have the court determine the identity of the father-this determination will be made using genetic marker or DNA tests.

Financial Investigation: In order to determine a non-custodial parent's ability to pay child support, child support staff will attempt to determine the non-custodial parent's income and assets. This is completed through inquiries to employers and banks, and computer searches of the files of the State Wage Reporting System (WRS), the New Hire Reporting System (New Hires), and information received from the State Department of Taxation and Finance and the Internal Revenue Service.

Support Establishment: Local child support staff will assist custodial parents in filing a petition with the Family Court in order to obtain a child support order. Information regarding the non-custodial parent's ability to pay is presented to the court for use in calculating the support amount. The court uses a standard guideline to figure out what the non-custodial parent will pay. The child support amount is based, in part, on the non-custodial parent's adjusted gross income and in part on how many children are involved. The court first determines the non-custodial parent's gross income, and then deducts from the gross income Medicare, social security tax, local and state taxes, and other allowable deductions to establish the non-custodial parent's adjusted gross income. The court then multiplies the adjusted gross income by the standard guideline percentage for the number of children. Generally, these percentages are approximately:
* 17% for one child,
* 25% for two children,
* 29% for three children,
* 31% for four children,
* at least 35% for five or more children.

In each case, a share of childcare, medical, and educational expenses is added to the appropriate percentage amount. Together, the combined amount is the basic child support amount.

The standard guideline percentage is applied to almost all parental earnings up to $80,000 (minus certain local and social security tax amounts). This includes worker's compensation, disability payments, unemployment benefits, social security payments, and many other forms of income. After $80,000, the court determines whether or not to use the percentage guidelines, and it may consider other factors in setting the full support award.

Support Collection: The child support order will require the non-custodial parent to send all child support payments to the local Child Support Enforcement Unit's Support Collection Unit (SCU). In order to keep track of payments, the SCU will build a computerized account, which will keep track of how much child support is due, and the frequency at which it is due.

If the non-custodial parent's employer is known, a notice called an income execution (IEX) will be sent to the employer notifying them of the amount of child support that should be taken from the non-custodial parent's wages and where the child support money should be sent. If an employer is not known, the non-custodial parent will receive billing coupons that will indicate the amount due, when the payment is due, and where payments should be mailed.

The SCU is also responsible for mailing checks to custodial parents. Thus, when a payment is received by the SCU, the SCU will send a check to the custodial parent. If the custodial parent is on temporary or safety net assistance, the first $50 of current support collected during the month will be sent to the custodial parent-this is called a support *pass-through* payment. The remainder of the money received from the noncustodial parent will be used to reimburse the local, state, and federal government for temporary or safety net assistance paid to the custodial parent.

Support Enforcement—Administrative Process: Administrative enforcement processes are those actions that the child support agency can complete without going to court. These actions include:
* Income execution
* Unemployment insurance intercept
* Income tax refund offset
* Credit bureau submissions
* Lottery intercepts
* Property execution
* Driver's license suspension
* Passport denial
* Lien filing
* Tax referrals

Before any administrative enforcement action is taken, a notice will be sent to the non-custodial parent that explains the process, provides a timeframe and instructions for complying or challenging the action, and provides the consequences that will result from a failure to comply with the payment instruction. Numerous enforcement actions may occur at the same time based on the amount of debt owed or the length of time the debt has been building up (accruing).

Support Enforcement-Court based: When administrative enforcement processes are unsuccessful, the SCU will assist in preparing and filing a violation petition with the court requesting that the court enforce the order. The court can: order mandatory money judgments for the arrears; order the non-custodial parent into a work program; order that a hearing take place to suspend state issued professional, business or occupational licenses; or issue probation or jail sentences.

Medical Support Establishment and Enforcement: The CSEU will also assist the custodial parent in obtaining and enforcing a court order for health insurance coverage for the child, if it is available through the non-custodial parent. The CSEU will help file a petition with Family Court to get health insurance included in the support order and will enforce the coverage if it is available through the noncustodial parent's employer, but has not been provided as ordered.

Modification of Child Support Orders: Either parent or the CSEU can file a petition in Family Court to request a modification (change) to an existing child support order. The modification petition should be based on the fact that either the custodial or non-custodial parent's circumstances have materially changed (e.g., change in income, or other changes in circumstances).

Cost of Living Adjustment: Every two years the child support agency automatically reviews each child support order to determine whether the amount to be paid should be increased due to cost of living increases. If the cost of living has increased by more than ten percent since the order was made or since the last review, the child support order amount will increase by the amount that the cost of living changed. The cost of living adjustments can be made without going to court. For non-temporary assistance or non-safety net cases, a notice is sent to both parents when a case is eligible for a cost of living adjustment, and either parent may request the adjustment. For cases where the custodial parent or child is on temporary or safety net assistance, the cost of living adjustment is automatically made when the case becomes eligible-without either parent requesting the adjustment.

FINANCIAL INVESTIGATIVE TERMS

Glossary

This glossary contains terms presented in the text as well as terms which may be brought out in discussion.

Account
An accounting device used in recording the day-to-day changes in revenue, expense, asset, liability, and owner's equity items.

Account, nominal. Temporary account for an item appearing on an income statement and closed to a balance sheet account at the end of an accounting period.

Account, real. Account for an item appearing on a balance sheet.

Accounting
The system of recording and summarizing business and financial transactions in books and analyzing, verifying, and reporting the results.

Accounting, cost. The process of collecting material, labor, and overhead costs and attaching them to products.

Accounting Period
The period of time over which the transactions of a business are recorded and at the end of which a financial statement is prepared.

Account Payable
An obligation to pay an amount to a creditor.

Account Receivable
An amount that is owed to the business, usually by one of its customers, as a result of the ordinary extension of credit.

Account Transactions
Financial events that directly affect the movement of money through a bank account.

Accrual Basis of Accounting
Recording business revenues when they are earned, regardless of when they are collected, and recording expenses when they are incurred, regardless of when cash was disbursed.

Accrued Expenses
Expenses incurred but not yet paid for.

Accrued Income
Income earned but not yet received.

Adjusting Entry
Recording the correction of an error, accruals, write-offs, provisions for bad debts or depreciation, etc., expressed in the form of a simple journal entry.

Affiant
The person who prepares an affidavit.

Affidavit
A handwritten or typed declaration or statement of facts made voluntarily and confirmed by the oath or affirmation of the party making it before an officer having authority to administer such oath.

Alien Corporation
Corporation of another nationality operating in the United States.

Amortize
To write off a portion or all of the cost of an intangible asset.

Appraise
Cash or value established by systematic procedures that include physical examination, pricing, and often engineering estimates.

Asset
Property or resources owned by a business or individual.

Asset, current. An asset which is either currently in the form of cash or is expected to be converted into cash within a short period, usually one year.

Asset, fixed. Tangible property of relatively long life that generally is used in the production of goods and services.

Association Matrix
The graphic summary that results from link analysis.

Audit
A critical review of a business's accounting records.

Bad Debts
Accounts that are considered to be uncollectible.

Balance, Beginning
The amount in an account at the start of the accounting period.

Balance, New
The amount in an account at the end of the accounting period, it is the difference between the beginning balance plus increases and minus decreases.

Balance Sheet
A financial statement that reports the assets, liabilities, and equities of a company as of a specified time.

Balance Sheet consolidated. Aggregate accounts for the various categories of assets and liabilities of a corporate family (more than one corporation).

Bank Deposit Method
An indirect method of proving unknown sources of funds through an analysis of bank records and other financial transactions entered into by a suspect.

Bank Reconciliation
A comparison of the customer's records with the records of the bank, listing differences to bring balances into agreement.

Bank Statement
A document rendered by the bank to the depositor, usually monthly, which reflects deposits and checks which have cleared the bank.

Blackmail
A demand for money or other considerations under threat to do bodily harm, to injure property, to accuse of crime, or to expose disgraceful defects.

Bond

Any interest bearing or discounted government or corporate security that obligates the issuer to pay the bondholder a
specified sum of money, usually at specific
intervals, and to repay the amount of the loan at maturity.

Bond, corporate. A bond issued by a private corporation.

Bond, coupon. A bond that has coupons attached to the bond certificate, one coupon for each interest payment due during the life of the bond. The interest is payable to whoever turns in the coupon, whether or not that person initially bought the bond.

Bond, municipal. A bond issued by a state, county, municipality, or any agency thereof
Bond, registered. A bond where the name of the owner appears on the bond certificate. Interest on the bond is paid by check directly to the registered holder.

Bond, registered coupon. A bond where the name of the owner appears on records maintained by a registrar and/or transfer agent. The interest coupons attached to the bond certificate do not contain the name of the owner and are payable to the bearer. Registered coupon bonds are registered for the principal only, not for interest.

Bribery
When money, goods, services, information, or anything else of value is offered with the intent to influence the actions, opinions, or decisions of the taker.

Bylaws
The rules adopted by the stockholders setting forth the general method by which the corporate functions are to be carried on subject to the corporate charter.

Case Law
The practice of judges and lawyers looking into decisions from past cases to determine the state of law for the case they are currently handling.

Cash Basis of Accounting
Recording business revenues when cash is received and business expenses when cash is paid.

Cash Flow
The cash flow calculation attempts to measure the actual cash receipts and cash expenses of a firm.

Cashier's Check
A check drawn by a bank on its own funds and issued by an authorized officer of the bank.

Certified Check
A check where the bank guarantees that there are sufficient funds on deposit for that particular check.

Chart of Accounts
A listing, in sequentially numbered order, of a business's accounts.

Civil Law
That body of law that deals with conflicts and differences between individuals.

Closed Corporation
Corporation owned by a few stockholders, not available for investment by public.

Codification
The process of collecting and arranging laws by subject.

Collateral
Something of value pledged as security for a loan.

Common Law
The system of law that originated in England and was the body of law carried by the earliest English settlers to the American colonies.

Contingency
A possible future event or condition arising from causes unknown or at present undeterminable.

Contra Account
One of two or more accounts which partially or wholly offset each other. On financial statements, they may either be merged or appear together, for example, an account receivable from and payable to the same individual.

Cooperative
A corporation in which profits are distributed to shareholders in proportion to the amount of business each shareholder does with the company.

Counterfeiting
Copying or imitating an item without having been authorized to do so and passing the copy off for the genuine or original item.

Corporation
An artificial being or business entity created under state or federal law which is legally separate from the persons who own it.
Ownership is in the form of stock and the liability of the owners is limited to the amount of their investment in the company.

CR
Abbreviation of credit.

Credit Entry
An entry on the right-hand side of a T-account.

Creditor
One who lends money.

Criminal Law
That branch of law that deals with offenses of a public nature, that is, wrongs committed against the state.

Cartilage
The area inside the boundary of a person's residence or business location which has been marked off by man-made or naturally-occurring devices.

Debit Entry
An entry on the left-hand side of a T-account.

Debt
Current and non-current liabilities.

Defalcation
The embezzlement of money.

Depreciation
The expiration of an asset's "quality of usefulness."

Discount Amount by which the face value of a financial investment exceeds the sales price.

Dividend
Portion of a company's profits distributed to stockholders.

Dividend, cash. Dividend paid in the form of cash.

Dividend, property. Dividend paid in the form of stock from another corporation.

Dividend, stock. Dividend paid in the form of shares of stock in the issuing corporation.

Domestic Corporation
A corporation doing business in the state from which it received its charter.

Double Entry Accounting
The type of accounting in which the two aspects of each financial event are recorded.

DR
Abbreviation of debit.

Draft
An order in writing directing the payment of money by one party (the drawee) to another party (the payee). A bank check is an example of a draft.

Electronics Fund Transfer
A transaction with a financial institution by means of a computer, telephone, or electronic instrument.

Elements of a Crime
Those constituent parts of a crime that must be proven to sustain a conviction.

Elements of a Crime
Those constituent parts of a crime that must be proven to sustain a conviction.

Embezzlement
When one entrusted with money or property appropriates it for his or her own use and benefit.

Entry, Closing
An entry reducing one account to zero and offset by an entry increasing another account by the same amount. It is one step in transferring the balance of an account to another account.

Equity, Owner's
Claims against assets by the owner(s).

Evidence
Anything that can make a person believe that a fact or proposition is true or false.

Evidence, circumstantial. Evidence relating to a series of facts other than those at issue that tend, by inference, to establish the fact at issue.

Evidence, direct. Evidence precise to the point at issue.

Evidence, documentary.

Evidence in the form of writings and documents.

Evidence, real. Evidence that is tangible.

Evidence, testimonial. Evidence given by word of mouth.

Exemplar
Non-testimonial identification evidence from a defendant, such as a blood or handwriting sample.

Expenditure
Payment for acquiring an asset or service.

Expenditures Method
An indirect method of determining unknown sources of funds by comparison of all known expenditures with all known receipts during a particular period of time.

Expense
Goods or services consumed in operating a business.

Expense, accrued. A liability account arising from expenses that are incurred prior to the related expenditure, for example, accrued wages.

Expense, prepaid. An expense recognized after a relevant expenditure, for example, future benefits.

Extortion
Illegally obtaining property from another by actual or threatened force, fear, or violence, or under cover of official right

Felony
A serious crime punishable by incarceration for a period exceeding one year, a fine, and the loss of certain civil rights.

Financial Condition
The results conveyed by presenting the assets, liabilities, and capital of an enterprise in the form of a balance sheet. Sometimes called financial position.

Financial Interviewing
The systematic questioning of persons who have knowledge of events, those involved, and evidence surrounding a case under investigation.

Fiscal Year
An accounting period of twelve successive calendar months.

Foreign Corporation
A corporation with a charter from another state. A California corporation doing business in Nevada is a foreign corporation in Nevada.

Forensic Science
The application of scientific techniques to legal matters.

Forgery
Passing a false or worthless instrument, such as a check or counterfeit security, with the intent to defraud or injure the recipient.

Forfeiture
A legal proceeding that the Government initiates against the proceeds of an illegal activity.

Fraud
Falsely representing a fact to another in order to induce that person to surrender something of value.

General Partner
A partner personally liable for partnership debts.

Goodwill
An intangible asset representing the difference between the purchase price and the value of the tangible assets purchased.

Grand Jury
A jury who hears evidence obtained by the prosecution and then decides whether or not a trial ought to occur.

Guarantor
One who promises to make good if another fails to pay or otherwise perform an assigned or contractual task.

Hearsay
Evidence that does not come from the personal knowledge of the declarant but from the repetition of what the declarant has heard others say.

Hybrid Method
Method of accounting which is a combination of the cash and accrual methods.

Immunity
An investigative tool used by the grand jury that allows a witness to provide testimony or documents without fear of prosecution.

Income Statement
A financial statement showing revenues earned by a business, the expenses incurred in conducting business, and the resulting net income or net loss.

Income, Net
Excess of total revenues over total expenses in a given period.

Indictment
A formal written complaint of criminal charges.

Indirect Methods
Ways of proving unknown or illegal sources of funds which rely upon circumstantial evidence.

Informant
A person who has specific knowledge of a criminal event and provides that information to a law enforcement officer.

Insider Trading
Using "inside" or advance information to trade in shares of publicly held corporations.

Intangible Asset
Any nonphysical asset, such as goodwill or a patent, which has no physical existence. Its value is dependent on the rights that possession confers upon the owner

Interest
Charge for the use of money.

Interrogation
Questioning of suspects and/or uncooperative witnesses for the purpose of obtaining testimony and evidence or proof of significant omissions.

Interview
A specialized form of face-to-face communication between people that is entered into for a specific task-related purpose associated with a particular subject matter.

Inventory
Goods being held for sale, and material and partly finished products, which upon completion, will be sold.

Investment Banker
A person or company in the business of marketing bonds and stocks for a corporation desiring to raise money

Invoice
Bill for goods delivered or services rendered.

Journal
A book of original entry in which transactions are initially recorded before being posted to a ledger.

Judicial Notice
When a court recognizes the existence and truth of certain facts.

Kickback
When a person who sells an item pays back a portion of the purchase price to the buyer or public official.

Lapping
The substitution of checks for cash received. A term used in embezzlement schemes.

Larceny
Wrongfully taking another person's money or property with the intent to appropriate, convert, or steal it.

Law
A formal means of social control intended to guide or direct human behavior toward ends that satisfy the common good.

Ledger
An accounting device used to summarize journal entries by specific accounts.

Lessee
The person or company possessing and using a leased item.

Lessor
The person or company holding legal title to a leased item.

Letter of Credit
A document issued by a bank authorizing designated banks to make payments on demand to a specified individual up to a stated total amount.

Liability
A debt owed.

Liability, current. Obligation that becomes due within a short time, usually one year.

Liability, long-term. Obligation with maturity dates more than one year after the balance sheet date.

Line of Credit
A commitment by a bank to a borrower to lend money at a stated interest rate for a stated period

Link Analysis
A technique for evaluating, integrating, and presenting complex information collected from various sources and putting them together to show patterns and meanings.

Liquidity
Ability to meet current obligations.

Loss, Net
Excess of total expenses over total revenue in a given period.

Mala In Se
Crimes that are said to be evil or immoral in and of themselves.

Mala Prohibita
Offenses that are made criminal by statute but in and of themselves are not necessarily immoral.

Maturity of Loan
The due date of a loan.

Memorandum
A written record of an interview embodying something that an investigator desires to fix in memory.

Moms Rea
A legal term meaning proof of criminal intent.

Misdemeanor
Crimes less serious than felonies that are punishable by incarceration for a period of less than one year and/or a fine.

Money Laundering
The process by which one conceals the existence, illegal source, or legal application of income and then disguises that income to make it appear legitimate.

Money Order
A negotiable instrument that serves as a substitute for a check.

Mutual Company
Type of corporation that has no stockholders, but is owned by its customers.

Net Worth
The excess of asset value over creditor claims; Assets Liabilities = Net Worth (Equity).

Net Worth Method
An indirect method of proving unknown sources of funds by comparing net worth at the beginning and end of specified period of time.

Note
A written promise to repay a loan.

Note Receivable
A debt that is evidenced by a note or other written acknowledgment.

Open Corporation
A corporation whose stock is available for investment by the public.

Partner
One of the owners of an unincorporated business.

Par Value
A specified amount printed on the face of a stock certificate.

Partnership
A company created when two or more individuals agree to do business together.

Percentage Method
An indirect method of proving unknown sources of funds by using percentages or ratios considered typical of a business under investigation.

Physical Inventory, Taking of
Counting all merchandise on hand, usually at the end of an accounting period.

Posting
Transfer of an entry from a journal to a ledger account.

Probable Cause
All the facts and circumstances within the knowledge of an investigator about a criminal activity that can be considered reasonable and trustworthy.

Proceeds
Whatever is received when an object is sold, exchanged, or otherwise disposed of.

Profit and Loss Account
A temporary account where revenue and expense accounts are transferred at the end of an accounting period.

Profit, Gross
Sales minus cost of goods sold.

Proof
The establishment of a fact by evidence.

Proprietor
The owner of an unincorporated business.

Proprietorship
A business owned by one person who is usually both the manager and the owner.

Prospectus
A summary of a corporation registration statement designed to inform a prospective purchaser of securities. It must contain a fairly extensive disclosure statement of essential facts pertinent to the security.

Question and Answer Statement
A complete transcript of the questions, answers, and statements made by each participant during an interview.

Questioned Document
A document that has been questioned in whole or in part in respect to its authenticity, identity, or origin.

Racketeering
Running an illegal business for personal profit.

Reasonable Doubt
The degree of certainty a person has in accomplishing or transacting the more important concerns in everyday life.

Registration Statement
A statement describing, in detail, the financial condition of a corporation, its business, and the reasons it proposes to offer an issue of stocks or bonds to the public.

Revenue
An increase in owner's equity arising from operations.

Search Warrant
A written order by a judge or magistrate, it describes the place to be searched as well as the items to be seized.

Security
A stock, bond, note, or other document that represents a share in a company or a debt owed by a company or government entity.

Shell Corporation
A corporation that has no assets or liabilities, simply a charter to do business.

Single-Entry Accounting
A system of accounting that makes no effort to balance accounts.

Silent Partner
A partner not liable for debts of the partnership beyond the amount of his or her investment in the partnership and who does not participate in management. Also known as a limited partner.

Stakeout
A common term for stationary surveillance.

Sting
A short-term undercover operation.

Stock
Ownership of a corporation represented by shares that are a claim on the corporation's assets and earnings.

Stock, capital. Stock that is authorized by a company's charter.

Stock, common. Units of ownership in a company that allow the owner to receive dividends on his or her holdings.

Stock, issued. The number of shares of stock actually sold or distributed by a corporation.

Stock, outstanding. Issued stock less treasury stock.

Stock, preferred. The class of stock entitled to preferential treatment with regard to dividends or with regard to the distribution of assets in the event of liquidation.

Stock, treasury. Shares of stock issued and subsequently reacquired by the corporation.

Stock Certificate
A document evidencing ownership in a corporation.

Stockholders
An owner of an incorporated business with the ownership being evidenced by stock certificates.

Stock Split
An exchange of the shares outstanding for two or more times their number.

Subpoena
A document that requires a witness to appear before a grand jury or requires the witness to produce records and documents for the grand jury.

Substantive Law
The body of law that creates, discovers, and defines the rights and obligations of each person in society.

Surplus, Capital
An increase in owner's equity not generated through the company's earnings.

Surveillance
The secretive and continuous observation of persons, places, and things to obtain information concerning the identity and activity of individuals suspected of violating criminal laws.

T-Account
An accounting device used for recording increases and decreases on either side of vertical line, with account title on the top.

Tax Evasion
Committing fraud in filing or paying taxes.

Torts
A terms used in civil law, it refers to the private wrongdoings between individuals.

Transaction
The exchange of goods and services.

Treasury Bill
A short-term security offered by the U.S. Government with maturities of 13 weeks, 36 weeks, and 52 weeks.

Treasury Bond
A long-term security offered by the U.S. Government with maturities of 10 years or longer.

Treasury Note
An intermediate-term security offered by the U.S. Government with maturities from one to ten years.

Trial Balance
A list of the account balances arranged in "balance sheet order" by debits and credits with adjustment columns for entries. Used as a basis summary for financial statements.

Undercover Operation
An investigative tool where law enforcement officers or private individuals assume an identity other than their own for the purpose of gathering information relating to criminal violations.

Underwriter
A person or firm guaranteeing and usually participating in the marketing of securities to the public. The guarantee states the dollar amount the underwriter guarantees that the corporation will receive from the sale.

Underwriting Syndicate
A group of underwriters formed for the purpose of guaranteeing the successful sale of a particular issue of securities.

Unit and Volume Method
An indirect method of proving unknown or illegal sources of funds by applying price or profit figures to the known quantity of business.

United States Code
A multi-volume publication of the text of statutes enacted by Congress.

Voucher System
A control system within a company for cash payment.

Worksheet
An accounting device used to organize accounting data.

www.ingramcontent.com/pod-product-compliance
Lightning Source LLC
Chambersburg PA
CBHW082041300426
44117CB00015B/2559